BARRY WATERS

Totally Piste

THE ULTIMATE GUIDE TO SURVIVAL SKIING

Totally Piste

BARRY WATERS

THE ULTIMATE GUIDE TO SURVIVAL SKIING

ILLUSTRATED BY GRAHAM THOMPSON

PELHAM BOOKS

Also by Barry Waters

Piste Again
Back on the Piste
The Tennis Racket
Wish We Weren't Here: A Survival Guide to Abroad
Squash Balls
Between the Sheets: A Survival Guide to Sailing

PELHAM BOOKS

Published by the Penguin Group
27 Wrights Lane, London W8 5TZ, England
Viking Penguin Inc., 40 West 23rd Street, New York, New York 10010, USA
Penguin Books Australia Ltd, Ringwood, Victoria, Australia
Penguin Books Canada Ltd, 2801 John Street, Markham, Ontario, Canada L3R 1B4
Penguin Books (NZ) Ltd, 182–190 Wairau Road, Auckland 10, New Zealand

Penguin Books Ltd, Registered Offices: Harmondsworth, Middlesex, England

First published in 1988

Printed and bound in Great Britain by Butler and Tanner, Frome
Typeset by Goodfellow & Egan in 11/12½ Korinna.

A CIP catalogue record for this book is available from the British Library.

ISBN 0 7207 184 0 6

CONTENTS

Introduction
1 The Snow Show 1
2 Putting it Together 11
3 Slopemanship 16
4 Instruction 22
5 Selecting Your Instructor 35
6 Training Your Tutor 43
7 Gear 46
8 On The Level 53
9 Summer Skiing 59
10 Snow Wars 63
11 Après-Ski 71
12 Summit Meetings 77
13 Skiing Double 83

For Christina

INTRODUCTION

**'Here we are again,
with both feet planted firmly in the air'**

Trade Union leader, Hugh Scanlon

Hugh Scanlon was actually talking about the Common Market. But his remarks could equally well have applied to skiing, which is something else that Brits seem to have got roped into against their better judgement. And, as with the EEC, there is no immediate sign of our opting out.

Every year, more and more of us are to be found freezing our assets on the high ground, crossing skis with bad-tempered foreigners in the lift queue in a vain effort to prove to ourselves that there is life after birth. Instead of staying sensibly at home and catching a cold, we head for another extreme experience at Ice Station Zebra and catch pneumonia. Clad in our brightly coloured romper suits, feet jammed into those steel traps, we set off down assorted heart-stopping precipices like misguided missiles on what may well prove to be a one-way ticket to (ski)Boot Hill. Even if we did manage to get out a cry of 'Help', our words would probably freeze in the air.

What is it about The Big Chill, Monster Mountains and the possibility of sudden death that turn us on? Surely people have realised by now that Life at the Top means no more than High Anxiety. Or even worse: it's not just bone-*chilling* up there, it also can be bone-*breaking*.

Far from leaving your troubles behind, they are only just beginning. Even the law says that skiing is a 'dangerous sport'. And there's no question that it ought to be issued with a government health warning – not so much because it's dangerous though, but because it's *addictive*. Nevertheless, even if we are plonkers on planks rather than poetry in motion, and the highest we really want to go is the third floor of Lillywhites (to buy all that snazzy gear) we are still getting hooked in ever-increasing numbers. There are even weekends when Ski Sunday gets a bigger audience than Match of the Day.

Deep down inside, of course, we all know that if God had wanted us to ski he would have given us long feet; that man is a warm-blooded animal; that just because people were sliding around on boards 2,000 years ago doesn't mean it's natural; that skiing is the ultimate trivial pursuit and one sure way of saying goodbye very quickly to all the money stuffed into our zip-fastened trouser pockets.

Nonetheless, this hasn't stopped vast numbers of Brits from getting twitchy knees at the onset of winter; starting to walk up stairs instead of taking the lift; muttering to themselves skiing prayers like 'Blessed are the piste-makers' and 'Snow Snow, Quick, Quick Snow'; and wondering whether to invest in a four-wheel drive.

Perhaps it's just the snob appeal of it all. There is no question that skiing is a very snowcial sport and that snowbberry abounds on the slopes. So spending some time being downwardly mobile seems to have become a *sine qua non* for the 'upwardly mobile' or for those with aspirations to High Snowciety. Even the Pope skis, not to mention the Royals.

Whatever the reason, there would appear to be no stopping it. There is snow hiding place. So for the moment we are going to have to learn to live with it and make the best of things. It was with this objective that almost a decade ago this author wrote that classic handbook for hesitant skiers, *Piste Again*, in the belief that 'most skiers are not that young any more, don't like heights or snow, would be upset if they broke a leg, and just want to get through the day with a flush on their cheeks, a few tales to tell and their skiing ego intact'. It suggested a few ways and wiles (otherwise known as the techniques of 'Survival Skiing' or 'piste de résistance') to help reluctant piste bashers to survive, and occasionally even to *succeed* on the slopes – showing them how to cope with 'the high life' until the ski boom died away. 'Eddie The Eagle' has, of course, since shown the world that lack of ability need be no barrier to success on the slopes.

The fact is, however, (even though *Piste Again* is the name of one of the newest discotheques in Gstaad and is still being sported on t-shirts) that *Piste Again*, and its companion volume *Back on the Piste*, have not kept pace with

events. Far from fading away, skiing has kept on developing: new instruction techniques; a revolution in gear; more advanced forms of hooliganism in the snow wars between different nationalities on the slopes; the boom in summer skiing and in cross-country skiing; and much else besides.

Hence the need for yet another volume in the *Piste* series to bring Survival Skiers right up to date with all the latest wheezes for getting by on the slopes, and giving them some advance warning of what they may be letting themselves in for this season. So if you're in any doubt whether fluffy earmuffs are in or out; if you aren't sure that 'ski sauvage' is quite your style; if powder for you is the 'Johnson's Baby' variety; if your skis don't exactly 'kiss' the snow; if you prefer to ski with the handbrake on; if you'd rather contribute to the black economy than the white economy; if you only sidestep up the slope when there's a worthwhile objective (like a café), this book may be for you. Plank-hopping is never going to be completely painless, but with the help of *Totally Piste*, you should have the 'snow how' to ensure that your skiing is pretty much all downhill, and that, at least, you return with your limbs all present and correct.

○ RESORTS

The snow reports in the newspapers will bear no relation to the conditions when you arrive

If they say it's *possible* to ski back to the hotel, that doesn't mean it's possible *for you*

Ten minutes walk from the lifts does not mean ten minutes in your ski boots

If the bus is free it won't be frequent

The year the weather is really bitter is the year you will have chosen a high resort with North-facing slopes

The 'basic holiday price' is approximately one third of what it will actually cost

The duvet is never long enough

1 THE SNOW SHOW

**'The idea is to look like a cross between subway graffiti
and Papua New Guinea. The skier, even at a dead stop,
will snap, sizzle and smoke.'**

Martie Sterling, American writer
on 1987/88 winter fashions

Times change. It's not actually so long ago that almost the only colour worn on the slopes was regulation navy blue – though you did see the occasional flash Harry in black with a white sweater. In *Piste Again*, of course, we did recommend the 'old-timer' look – getting yourself up like the old hand who knows his way around. These days, however, designer-dressing is the norm – even for budget-buying Brits; and rambling on nostalgically about leather boots and cable bindings can make even the Survival Skier seem a bit too long in the tooth. You can all too easily find yourself boring the salopettes off your younger skiing companions. Thus an increasing number of Survival Skiers have decided to update their act and invest in the sort of rig which now passes for style on the slopes.

This need not be, it should be noted, what the ski fashion pundits have decided is this year's 'in' look or this month's 'ultimate' Space Age material. The fact is that everyone has so many ski outfits these days that no one on the slopes has any idea what is *this* year's look, what is *last* year's and what is *next* year's.

So the Survival Skier can safely ignore 'the new look' being pushed by yet another ex-skiing champ who is now wowing them with his zany line in gear rather than his line down the slopes. These garments, needless to say, will all be made of a new fifth generation silicone wonderfibre that is thirty per cent warmer, diamond-tough, accelerates faster and insulates as it breathes. (This actually means that the manufacturers have found yet another way of making nylon or polyester and a new type of synthetic filling to do what goose or duck down used to do. But by making it sound revolutionary enough, they can charge more for something that's cheaper to make.)

This new material will inevitably be run up by the ex-champ's little Japanese designer in Paris who this season will perhaps have decided that we should all be in sherbert and cerise billowy one-piece wraparounds – with magenta and fuchsia tail-drapes to show off our slipstreams. That's for the chaps, of course. For the girls he's come up with a little prison grey number cut like a pair of battle fatigues and decorated with alphabet soup and quadratic equations.

Survival Skiers, however, would do better to dress dangerously in styles of *their own* choosing. Ideally your outfit should look as if you put it together yourself and should always include various bits and pieces that apparently have a special significance for you (like that blood-stained bandanna you were left clutching when your friend slipped down a crevasse). You might also wear an item or two that are somewhat impractical (e.g. fur gloves, leather trousers) since this does rather tend to proclaim that you ski well enough to get away with it (i.e. you don't fall).

This sort of approach should make at least as much of an impression as the latest designer one-piece with all the accessories coordinated. But, do bear in mind, that, like the ex-champ's, your gear also should 'go for it' – if only to distract attention from your rather less than intrepid skiing. Remember – snow business is show business. Skiing is a high visibility sport (occasional blizzards and whiteouts notwithstanding). Not for nothing are those bindings called 'Look'.

Dressing up is also part of the fun – even though it can take you all morning to peel on one of those 'second-skin' fluorescent Lycra racing suits. (Not a bad bet, actually, for the Survival Skier who likes to take his time before appearing on the slopes.) And the gear does give you a sense of security – we feel protected somehow in those seven-league boots and padded clothes.

In order to make an impact (apart from when you collide with other skiers) the Survival Skier should bear very much in mind *where* he'll be skiing. Thus, for example, at a serious Swiss resort, the Survival Skier will probably be dressed rather frivolously à la française, clowning around in laid-back gear, clutching a mono ski or one of this year's new ski 'toys' under his or her arm. (Survival Skiers, of course, can be of either sex – though for convenience we'll tend to use the masculine pronoun in this book.) At a French *station, par contre*, or amongst the Martini set, our Survival Skier will be kitted out with all the latest 'down to business' hi-tech gear worn by last season's racers. (Never mind if the equipment exceeds your skiing abilities – that's all part of the game.)

Most frequently, though, the Survival Skier's aim will be to look as if he doesn't take his skiing too seriously (which *might* explain some of his deficiencies in technique). So feel free to wear the sort of outfit that would look more at home in the disco, or perhaps something more sober, say a tweed coat. But even if you are going for the laid-back or uncoordinated look, do make sure you get all the details right.

Nothing the Survival Skier wears should be unplanned. Not that anyone – let alone a Survival Skier – will own up to all the time and effort they have put into their appearance, working on their chic technique rather than their ski technique. All the *talk*, both during ski and après, will be about skiing. You never *mention* the clothes. This is true even of the increasing number of resorts which have all but stopped any serious skiing and are now almost completely given over to posing and people-watching. (This is a phenomenon that had to come –

the fact is that there is not really enough time for both skiing and posing. You either dress to ski or ski to dress.)

It does help, though, if the Survival Skier knows how to make his way around the slopes, looking, for all the world, like a *real* skier. (Readers familiar with *Piste Again* will know the drill.) If ever you're curious, by the way, about how much skiing someone actually does, you can usually tell by just looking at their hands: the hands of the poseurs will be as tanned as their faces from all those hours spent lounging on the sundeck; the skiers' hands will be white since they've been wearing gloves most of the time. 'Banana' boots are another giveaway — showing you've spent more time walking around in your ski-boots than skiing in them.

You even keep your gloves on, of course, in spring or summer when skiing in swimwear — or even in the altogether (though this can be a bit expensive on the sun cream). Remember — these days — 'anything goes'. It's hard to imagine how much fuss Suzy Chafee caused all those years ago when she was photographed nude on skis for *The Sunday Times*. Today we've got to the point where, for

those who really want to maximise their all-over tan, a French designer has come up with a transparent ski suit made of a material which just lets through those tanning UV rays.

But although now anything goes, there's still a good deal of 'U' and 'non-U' attached to ski-clobber. And this can inhibit the Survival Skier who wants to cut a dash. What, for instance, will those little bobbly head antennae do for your image? Would you make a better impression with the latest double-glazed goggles, or with those wraparound tinfoil 'glasses' that seem to be all the rage? Should your gaiters be attached or detachable? And what kind of headband — wide or narrow, plaited or tubular, with eye-piece incorporated or not? And are those beer-can holders on the tips of your skis the way to win friends and influence people (or to get them under the influence)?

So, to give you an idea of what's 'in' and what's 'out' *at the moment*, here are a few pointers. But do bear in mind that things won't stay that way for long.

○ HEADGEAR ○

Most kinds of hat, including the red, white and blue so patriotically sported in the past by Prince Charles and others, are very *old hat*. If you are determined to wear something on your head, though, you might get away with a fur pillbox, quilted caps in prints and florals, or perhaps a tweed cap or Basque beret. And if you want to be dramatic, cowls or snoods are also absolutely OK.

What has come in to replace the hat is the headband in its many variations — wide, narrow, smooth, 'Fergie' furry, interknotted or flat, natural or synthetic, even in some cases, incorporating a peak. Some of the more exotic woollen ones are in fact not that far short of a hat. But they do still conform to the essential requirements of a headband: they stop your glasses from falling off, keep your ears from getting cold or getting sunburn, and — most important of all — *they don't ruin your hairstyle.* (Needless to say, they should not itch.)

Those fluffy earmuffs are not the thing at all anymore — though earmuffs combined with headband or incorporated with a Walkman earpiece or built on to your sunglasses are acceptable (and very useful if you want to avoid listening to other people's advice in the lift-queue).

○ SHADES ○

It's now glasses rather than goggles, worn on a leash or a multi-coloured coil cord around the neck. (Only Sloanes are still wearing them on the head.) Established brands are best — Ray Ban, Yves St Laurent, Bollé, Wayfarer. The classic 'catseye' Vuarnets tend to make you look a bit American — but they're OK *if white.* Mirrored lenses are giving way to tinted; and the shade of the lens is

4

probably now more important than the colour of the frame – and should be 'interesting'. (Try 'shooting' green or bronze.) Wraparounds and Porsche-style designs tend to look as if you are trying a bit too hard, as do visors on your sunglasses, high-altitude nose protectors and leather side shields. But, a pair of those American cult Oakleys with all their interchangeable bits and bobs is acceptable, as are those teeny 'sunbed' eye-pieces.

The Survival Skier, however, should try to make do *without* glasses – the macho 'crows-feet' look is rather in, and does avoid the 'panda' effect. But if you do stick to your shades, don't forget the demister. (This is perfect for the Survival Skier who needs to waste time – smearing it over his glasses, and then smearing it off again because he can't see through them.)

○ FACE ○

Women are now in full make-up and jewellery on the slopes (as indeed are some of the men). This, of course, means pearls for not a few Sloanes; lip-salve dangling on a neck cord for others. Avoid, however, those earrings and pendants with ski motifs, or shaped like ski sticks or whatever. Out, too, is the Black and White Minstrel look, with whitened lips and the splash of zinc on the nose (or piece of baco-foil). Instead, you should be using a neutral absorbent, high factor cream – it doesn't do to have a red or shiny nose. Lip gloss is very OK, though, as is technicolour 'war-paint'. If the weather turns nasty, a face-covering Balaclava is acceptable – but should be made of silk, cotton or very fine wool rather than the classic knit variety.

○ NECKWEAR ○

Try to go bare-throated if you can – thus extending your tan down as far as possible. The classic cotton roll-neck is still OK – *if worn unrolled*. But not those 'tubi-grip' affairs or 'neck-gaiters' – unless you can suggest that you often enough find yourself up to your ears in the powder. Bandannas or chequered Arafat-style Kaffiyehs are very much today's look – especially the big ones you can wrap around your neck several times and knot tight, rather than the loose front-knotted variety. Avoid the ones in the colours of the various Swiss cantons.

Scarves are also fine, provided they are *not* worn so much around the neck as just generally trailed about the body. The only exception to this is the little red (or sometimes yellow) scarf, with or without tassles, preferably made of cashmere. This should be worn tied at the front and tucked down your bib so as to be just visible at the throat when skiing. When you strip off at the restaurant, however, the Survival Skier can and *should* show rather more of it. (NB. The two ends should *not*, under any circumstances, descend lower than *nipple* height.)

○ TOPS ○

These should be loose, and preferably light and billowy so there's plenty of room for lots of other layers below. Just about anything will do – from a flak jacket to a balloon-silk windshirt; from a duffely poncho to a nightshirt; from a puffy jacket (or a real Puffa for Brits) to a windbreaker; from a flying jacket to a ski-shirt (preferably in a crinkly printed fabric); from a sweat-top to one of those fashionable ski-smocks (even though the top does tend to keep rubbing up against your nose). The best bet, though, for the Survival Skier, is to choose something that doesn't look as if it was designed for skiing. Whatever you wear, it should have plenty of flaps and tucks and folds and drapes and pleats, as well

as a sprinkling of rivets and press studs for good measure, and as many complicated pockets and zips (the longer the better) as possible – for all your little accessories.

Underneath you should have a fair old combination – sweatshirt, t-shirt, granpappy Yukon vest, lumberjack check flannel shirt, woollen waistcoat, or whatever. Just about anything will do, in fact, except a sweater (the ones in the traditional striped or Nordic design are a real no-no). Everything should be kept in place by your braces – very 'in' now and found in a variety of styles.

Unfortunately, it will not be possible to buy many of these garments without a logo or motif. But this should be as discreet as possible – perhaps a little egg (denoting your membership of one of the speed-skiing clubs – *or so you will say*). Avoid anything with a t-shirt slogan like: 'Skiers do it in the snow'; 'Piste Again'; 'Just because I sleep with you tonight doesn't mean I'll ski with you tomorrow'; 'I love Switzerland'; 'No problem'; 'Summer stinks – Think Snow'; 'Eat my powder, suckers'. Worst of all is probably the name, or even logo, of your chalet company. You might, however, get away with something like 'Vasaloppet 1982'. Anoraks autographed by assorted championship skiers are also very much out.

Remember, too, that everything on your jacket should be detachable and discardable – sleeves, cuffs, pockets – so that it can speedily be converted into a natty little gilet. (When you do cast off your sleeves, though, don't forget to hang on to the goggle-strap watch on your upper arm – very 'in' these days.)

Be very careful, incidentally, about plumping for unknown Italian or American makes of anorak. Italians tend to have short bodies and Americans long arms. And neither the 'bum-freezer' look, nor the 'gorilla' look is very 'in' right now.

○ BOTTOMS ○

Stay well clear of salopettes – they're just too sensible. But you could try the sort of loose-fitting overalls that you might have borrowed from your local painter and decorator. If anything, though, there does seem to be a trend back to the traditional Keilhosen or stretch pants – with stirrups (for all those powder hounds). Few other garments since have shown off the line of the underbody quite so well. If, however, underbodies are not quite your line, why not try a pair of parachute pants or baggy trousers in natural materials, which make it look as if you've just walked in off the High Street. (This is totally impractical, of course, and so gives just the right effect.)

If you're in any doubt, though, you should be safe with Killy-cut trousers. Alternatively, try a bulky combination of over-trousers, trousers, and under-trousers, topped by multicoloured triple-decker gaiters. Another colour detail you might like to incorporate is the technicolour crotch, (reinforced if you ride a lot of Pomas) and contrasting with the rest of your outfit, that you can really show off when you take a tumble. (Not very often, of course, in *your* case.)

When the weather is warmer, you might try a pair of Bermudas or striped boxer-shorts – partly bare legs and arms (sleeves pushed up to your elbow) are very 'in'. (This is probably a development of the traditional type of ski wear where there was always a space at the top of your boots, and between your gloves and your sleeve, for the snow to accumulate.)

You should avoid blue jeans – unless you're a ski bum or a chalet girl, or can afford to wear them with a fur top. The fur, of course, should be *real*. There's more and more of it about on the slopes – mink head-bands, full length fur coats, even. So it's quite OK to work a bit of mink or reindeer trim onto your outfit.

The traditional one-piece jumpsuits and catsuits are still very much around – despite the difficulties of getting the top off for lunch and the bottom off *after* lunch. But they do tend to look a bit too designerish and tidy for the Survival Skier, whose aim is to look like his own designer.

One last touch that you might consider wearing down below is the knee brace. These are now being made in some rather snazzy colours and do make it look as if the Survival Skier has *earned* the right to take it a bit easier on the slopes these days.

○ GLOVES ○

These, of course, should be leather *not* vinyl, though some of the new hi-tech synthetics – in printed fabrics even – are OK. Wrists should be longish, perhaps gaiter-style (but not the half-sleeve glove, or detachable sleeve glove). If you really want to cut a dash – and are not too worried about frostbite – you could try a pair of those aerodynamic surgical gloves that the KL boys wear.

Avoid those sheepskin-lined gloves – they're a bit too pansified – though silk warmers underneath are OK. The Survival Skier should use electrically-heated gloves or 'warmpacks' *only if he must* – but do make sure no-one sees them. (This also goes for any other 'heated' ski garments.) Those blow tubes sticking out of your gloves, for instance, are an immediate giveaway.

On no account should you wear mittens – despite the advice given in so many British instruction manuals. (Try getting your lift pass out of your pocket with them.)

○ MATERIALS ○

Most of your clobber will probably be made of synthetic 'high performance' fabrics – *perhaps* treated so that you don't slide for half a kilometre when you fall. (The high gloss shiny look is back unfortunately.) But try to work as many natural materials as possible into your outfit – cotton, leather, wool, silk. The

latter is very much in — especially worn next to the skin — and is very easy to handwash overnight. (NB It's no longer done to wear the same underwear for a week's skiing — even if it is made of Chinese Imperial silk.) You might also try silk longjohns or those all-in-one 'scarlet teddies'. After all, the Survival Skier needs all the thermal insulation he can get.

The new man-made materials — Goretex, Thinsulate etc. — also do a pretty good job. But Survival Skiers concerned about their creature comforts should make sure that everything they wear has been tested in polar or Himalayan conditions. It goes without saying that this is unlikely to be the case with a good many of the more exotic 'in' designs — i.e. your pearlised zebra one-piece with leopard-skin trim, or your quilted satin blouson, or your Batik print shirt with appliqué finish.

○ COLOURS ○

Generally speaking, wear as many colours as possible — preferably clashing — unless you are going for the military drab effect. And try to make them as *interesting* as possible. The manufacturers do their best to help here by the names they give them — yellow becomes yolk or saffron; pink or cherry red is cerise, or even *orchard* cerise; orange becomes sunset; red becomes raspberry. Either that or there'll be an appropriate qualification — *peacock* blue, or *glacier* blue, or *ice* blue, or *pacific* blue.

○ LABELS ○

Preferably none. But since nothing can be bought without a manufacturer's logo, or a designer label these days, you'll probably have little choice. (Isn't it about time they started paying us to wear their brand names?)

The established brands like Ellesse, Killy, Belfe are still very much around. But you may score more points by supporting the challenge of one of the newer designers — Grosjean, Luhta, Schoeffel, Descente, Dubin, Mäser, Bognor (the man who came up with the first mink ski gilet). In this case, though, do be consistent — your sun-cream too should be Vichy rather than Boots.

○ HOLDALLS ○

The biggest change in recent years has been the demise of the bum-bag — with only the occasional Brit resisting the trend. Some people try to soldier on wearing their bum-bag *under* their jacket — for the 'Duck's Arse' effect. But this is not recommended.

Instead of the bum-bag, we have ski wear that consists of little else but pockets and miles of zips (preferably with plaket closure in front, or wind protector behind – unless you *like* air vents). As we've said, the Survival Skier can't be too careful.

Bags as such are not entirely out, however. Jazzy handbags, usually slung from the shoulder, made of fabric that matches your suit are making inroads, as is the belt pack (a sort of bum-bag in disguise), or the hat doubling as a bum-bag, or the bum-bag that's built into your clothes. Avoid, however, those kangaroo 'hidey' pouches or backpacks in the shape of Pandas or Koalas. If necessary, one of the standard types of rucksack is acceptable, or preferably, your own custom-made ski bag.

This should give you the general idea. But, of course, it's how you put it all together that counts. (See next chapter.) As we've seen, the key thing for the Survival Skier to remember is to *personalise* his or her outfit. There's no reason, however, why you shouldn't be practical about it. What about a panic button, for instance; or a snorkel (for powder skiing); or an oxygen mask (which you used for high skiing in the Himalayas); or a racing number tie-on (kept as a souvenir)? Other useful items are a snow-proof wallet (the Survival Skier often needs to dish out the odd backhander and to refuel on the mountain); a thermometer built into your anorak to keep tabs on the air temperature and wind chill factor (Survival Skiers can't be too careful – people have been known to die from hypothermia); an altimeter; and a well-padded behind for shock absorption or for 'sitting it out' till the weather improves. A pair of rubber knees can also come in handy.

○ MOUNTAINS

The mountain looks closer than it is

The mountain gets steeper as you get closer

It always looks steeper from the top than from the bottom

Skiing ability declines in inverse ratio to the proximity of the mountain

Whenever you stand and stare you can always see two people trekking uphill on a distant mountain-side

The day you set out to do the Vallée Blanche is the day you forget to bring your passport

At least once on every ski holiday you will think you are going to die alone on a deserted mountain-top and be brought down in a body-bag

---

2 PUTTING IT TOGETHER

'Later the Princess [Diana] spent the afternoon trying to ski incognito. She wore goggles, pulled her hat well down and turned up the collar of her fashionable ski suit in an attempt to hide her face. But then she fell full-length.'

Daily Telegraph report of the Prince and Princess of Wales' ski holiday in Liechtenstein

Now it is just possible that the previous chapter may have left you somewhat confused. But that, unfortunately, is the way the ski scene is tending to look at the moment. There are a tremendous number of different 'looks' around. To give you an idea of the range, here are some sketches of types you may well see around the slopes.

○ MICHELIN MAN (OR WOMAN) ○

One of the classics — the mobile duvet look once much favoured by British skiers who believed in lots of clothing worn under puffy ski suits bought a couple of sizes too big. (For a budget version, try stitching together some lagging from an old immersion heater.) A little bit impractical and dated, but perhaps an idea for the Survival Skier who prefers to sit it out at the *top* of the mountain. If you are prepared to go to the trouble of acquiring a genuine ex-NASA spacesuit complete with bubble helmet, you *may* make quite an impression.

○ SNOW WHITE ○

White belted body-hugging one-piece suit, preferably made by Event or some such, for the real snowbird. Usually a splash of colour somewhere though (probably red or yellow) just to make sure you don't miss her. In fact, she's probably about as pure as the driven slush — but you'd never guess it from the outfit.

○ RAMBO ○

The ultimate 'macho' look — for men *and* women. Not over-expensive either. You can find everything you need in your local army surplus store. Try parachute

pants and battle fatigues in camouflague colours, with khaki socks worn *outside* your boots. Head should be swathed in a bandanna, knotted behind, and trailing, which can also be used as a tourniquet or for binding up wounds.

○ SHEIK OF ARABY ○

Two versions of this. The upmarket djellabah-style top in cashmere or angora draped around you from the head down in folds — sort of 'Salome of Saas Fe'. Or, for the peasants, the Arafat-style dishcloth held in place by a headband — sort of Lawrence of Avoriaz. For a touch of the 'Mujehaddins', try the Vallencant look — flowing chiffon bandanna knotted at the back of the head and trailing.

○ SAILOR ○

Yellow wellies, puffa or anorak with drawstring hood, blue sailing style trousers, but perhaps padded for extra warmth. Not the most practical ensemble — but might just be one way of explaining why your skiing is not all that it might be — you're too busy on the boat for most of the year.

○ DRAPER ○

The key garment here is the long anorak-cum-coat. Can either be teddyboy three-quarter length or full length. Started off a few years ago with those long

quilted jackets worn very loose by the younger set. Now comes in a variety of materials — denim, gaberdine or whatever. Avoid, however, those fluorescent raincoats that are now making an appearance. For the right effect, this look should remind you of those longish coats they took to wearing in Sergio Leone spaghetti westerns. Should be worn with the right air of decadence.

○ ROCK STAR ○

Anything slinky, sexy, heavily crinkled in the right places (perhaps by your waist-nipping gold lamé belt), and generally totally inappropriate for the slopes. A Paisley shirt would do at a pinch, or perhaps a similar printed or star-spangled top in psychedelic colours. A suitable outfit perhaps for the Survival Skier who likes to ski by floodlight and then hop straight into the discotheque. Don't forget the bloodshot eyes to complete this look.

○ CROCODILE DUNDEE ○

Stetson, lumberjack shirt over polo neck — the traditional 'down-home' look favoured by American skiers. Or, for that extra something, leather fringed ski suit, or perhaps a reindeer-fur jacket or reindeer-skin legwarmers, and a husky in tow. Not really the thing in the Alps — unless you want to show you've been spending some time recently in that over-the-head Rocky Mountain powder.

○ MATA HARI ○

More one for the girls — but not exclusively so. Give yourself that air of mystery in sombre colours with a cowl over the head attached to a loose-fitting cloak-effect garment — all Dolmen drop-sleeves for that 'batwing' look, and plenty of material so that you can either drape it or wrap it around you.

○ APRÈS SKI ○

Any sort of après-piste outfit, but worn *on* the slopes — or on the sundeck. For the skier who makes no bones about his or her priorities. Big fur coats are one option — at the risk, for men, of being confused with Liberace, Nureyev or a male model. Expect to see a lot of developments in this look over the next few years as

13

après-ski gets closer and closer to ski. You can even find après-ski boots that slot into special bindings — but these can come a bit expensive.

○ **COURT JESTER** ○

Any sort of clowning-around harlequin outfit will do — perhaps a candy-striped or pirate-striped pair of baggy pants that bounce up and down on elasticated braces. At the other extreme, what about a sort of dinner jacket ensemble, with black bow tie worn on a bare neck?

○ **HEAVENLY TWINS** ○

Matching his and hers outfits, or even hers and hers, or even his and his — usually 'created' by one of the new designers. All a bit too twee — unless you can pair-ski as a coordinated duo, sort of Torvill and Dean on skis, in which case you *might* get away with it.

○ COMMANCHE ○

The Indian brave look – face streaked with primary-coloured splashes of zinc oxide face paint, usually on cheekbones and nose. (This comes off best if you're very brown. Spend some time under the sunlamp before coming out.)

○ TRAILER ○

Very 'in' this one. A look that has gradually evolved over the years. Used to be just the 'kerchief knotted around the thigh (most commonly red polka dot against a pair of faded blue jeans). Nowadays, though, you can let it all hang out. As much as possible should be worn undone and flapping. And there should be plenty of drawstrings, powder cords, leashes, bandannas, straps and rip cords 'trailing' in your slipstream. It does help if you can ski a bit so that you actually *have* a slipstream.

○ LIFTS

The one chair which is wet and which the attendant fails to brush the snow off will be yours

When you drop a stick or a glove from the chair-lift, it will always be while crossing the most inaccessible piece of terrain

The fact that a lift starts moving is no indication that anyone will be allowed to go up on it

This will not prevent a large queue from forming

The longer the queue the less likely the lift is to open

The jerk on a Poma only comes after you've stopped expecting it

The more unsteady the skier the more likely the lift attendant is to shovel snow onto the track ahead of him

If, according to your calculations, you are skiing at a speed that will enable you to cross just in front of or just behind someone going up a drag-lift, you have miscalculated

If you make a dash for the only lift that's still running, it will be closed the moment you get there

3 SLOPEMANSHIP

'Top Three? I think I'll finish in the top one.'

Olympic downhill gold-medallist, Bill 'Bigmouth' Johnson

Along with his outfit, the Survival Skier would do well to equip himself with some of the various types of 'toys', like sno-boards and so on, now to be found on the slopes in increasing numbers. These novelties have actually added a new dimension to the basic techniques of slopemanship which were outlined in *Piste Again*.

The Survival Skier should take advantage of the nervousness that most people feel about this gimmicky gear, and make them very much a part of his own repertoire. Less so, perhaps, in the up-to-the-minute French-style resorts, where you do find a number of people who actually know something about these things, but most emphatically when you find yourself in one of the traditional resorts.

The thing is that most skiers won't yet have tried them. (Memories of learning how to stagger about on standard equipment are probably still too painful in most cases.) This means the Survival Skier should be able to start 'one up'. He can probably even afford to roll up at the restaurant and park his monoski, or his funboard, or his wings, or his voile, or his parapente and confidently but casually invite his ski-chums to 'have a go': 'Go on. It's damned simple really' (though he might add warningly *once you get the hang of it*). If the Survival Skier has picked his crowd right, he almost certainly won't find any volunteers.

Problems may arise, of course, when the Survival Skier himself actually has to perform. Fortunately, both monos and ski-surfers are basically designed for the powder. So the Survival Skier can just confidently disappear off-piste well out of sight. After having spent an hour or so in some cosy little Hütte (preferably bewirtschaftet) he can then reappear on the piste. To allay any suspicions that people may have about what you've actually been doing, a little Father-Christmas cottonwool sprinkled liberally about your hair and body can make just the right impression from a distance. This will have 'melted' away, of course, by the time anyone gets to inspect you more closely. A bit of 'frosting' on the goggles is also a nice touch — try the sort of sugar and alcohol mix that you use for your pink gin.

The 'voile' and 'bird-sail' wings may pose more of a problem. But you can always busy yourself preparing the wings, fitting them to your poles, and folding and unfolding your voile, intermittently eyeing the mountaintops for a suitable

peak to sail off. Even better would be a proper army parachute if you can get hold of one — you can spend all day sorting it out. Easiest of all, though, are those mini-chutes you strap to your back and inflate by pulling a ripcord if you feel you are going to go under in an avalanche. They look rather forbidding, but provided you can get a bit of speed up, you can inflate at will and nothing too serious should happen.

With a bit of careful preparation, the skilled Survival Skier might even be able to persuade his admirers to look on him as a sort of latter-day Roger Moore in *For Your Eyes Only*, expecting at any moment that you will rocket off as you suddenly pop another toy. And, on the subject of rockets, how about getting hold of a pair of those turbo-powered skis the French are now working on for the 'Kilometre Pulsé'. In your fluorescent skin-tight suit and gigantic aerodynamic helmet you should make quite an impression with these. Hardly your fault that conditions are never right to 'run' them or that it might be a bit dangerous for others on such a crowded piste. You can always rev them up a couple of times to show onlookers what you mean.

One novelty to beware of perhaps are those plastic H-shaped plates that you fit to your ordinary skis to transform them into a monoski. It can be difficult to explain why you can't use these *on the piste*. This contraption, however, might

prove interesting to the Survival Skier who would like to experience *for once* — if only momentarily — the joys of actually skiing parallel.

Where you can really give yourself away with these things, as with monoskis, is trying to go up in a lift. Making your way through the queue will be quite a slog — whether you keep both boots in your bindings, or take one foot out to 'scooter' along. Once you're on the chair that 'strait-jacket' feeling from having your knees locked together as you go up can be very unsettling. And just try going up a drag lift on a mono or snurfboard with the button or T-bar jammed in your crotch — and threatening not to unjam if you fall off.

Something else you can give a miss are Scorpians (almost forgotten now) — although those half-metre long 'baby' skis are OK. (Why not just tuck a pair into your rucksack along with your biathlon rifle?) What can really cause a bit of a frisson at the restaurant is turning up in a bobsleigh (or, if you can't afford one, an old converted motor-cycle sidecar). Try and get up a bit of momentum for 20 metres or so as you approach the café (making sure there's a convenient *uphill* slope to run out on), and then climb out in your best devil-may-care manner, tether it like a horse to the sundeck railings and leap neatly on to the terrace, stripping off your helmet, and your elbow and kneepads. You can then proceed to regale the assembled company with tales of some of your more hair-raising experiences, and explain why you prefer bobsleighing to tobogganing down the Cresta: 'You need to be pie-eyed to toboggan well. I like to keep my wits about me.'

It's on such occasions that you can really install yourself at the restaurant, stripping off your Ski Patrol jacket so that people can admire your 'Dangerous Sports Club' t-shirt. No harm either in taking your boots and socks off in order to get really settled in. (But make sure your feet are well sprayed — you don't want to deter your audience.)

At other times, too, of course, Survival Skiers should make themselves comfortable at the restaurant, draping themselves and their gear around their deckchair. Then, by the time they've managed to get themselves together again, they'll be able to exclaim: 'Is that really the time — and I've got a squash court booked at 3.30' — thus absolving themselves of having to hit the slopes again.

It often pays to go to some length to establish the right sort of daredevil aura. You might, for instance, allow yourself to be seen one day hanging outwards by your knees from the hotel balcony (making sure, of course, that you have a couple of concealed and trustworthy collaborators holding onto your feet, which — to be on the safe side — should also be attached with climbing ropes).

You won't, incidentally, cut quite this sort of figure circling around the café in a snowmobile, or one of those mountain bikes with big knobbly tyres, or an electric buggy, or ski-bob, or even cruising around in your 4-wheel drive Audi Quattro, or Toyota Landcruiser. When it comes to these sort of vehicles, the Survival Skier will earn more admirers by leading the campaign for SSSH (Society for Silent Snowmobiles Here).

Far better to use your imagination and roll up on a piano, or a milkcrate, or a tin tray, or a bin-liner, or any number of other silly objects. In fact, this perhaps conveys best the sort of attitude the Survival Skier should have to the whole range of 'toys' currently on the market: 'alright for the kids', and 'for a bit of fun' — but not to be taken too seriously.

Many Survival Skiers might rather stay well away from such gimmickry altogether, preferring to rely on the time-honoured methods outlined in *Piste Again* for establishing their reputation around the slopes. Even these techniques, however, are being constantly refined by Survival Skiers just to keep ahead of the game. And although they may choose not to make use of the new 'toys', there are other props which they might well take advantage of.

If, for instance, your traverse is not as strong as it might be, one way of distracting attention from this deficiency is to glide around with a stopwatch in your hand and walkie-talkie nestling in your blouson (but clearly visible — aerial sticking up).

If even your traverse is pretty shaky and the snow plough is your limit, then perhaps the answer might be to display yourself ploughing down the slope carrying an enormous collection of ski gear and clobber explaining that 'your friends have changed into their mountaineering gear' — but climbing is 'not your

thing' any more since you took that tumble last year on the north face of the Eiger ('Good thing those sniffer dogs found me'); so you've volunteered to be a sort of Sherpa Tensing and take their ski gear back to the hotel (good fellow that you are). This ploy, of course, does require some investment in additional skis and clothes – though you might be able to just use an assortment of items from your own extensive wardrobe.

Another useful prop is one of those huge tripod-mounted stop-clocks that stand beside the starting gate at top races. Why not set one of these up on the piste, and then spend some time crouched low on the slope below 'tracing a race line' with your hands. A nice additional touch is to wrap up part of the clock box with one of 'your' old race tie-ons (marked, say, 'World Cup, Kitzbühel': 'So glad they gave me the old number 7 for the Streif last year – my lucky number').

Even with the 'just off piste' technique, you can make very good use of whatever props you have available. It's easy enough to rig up a kind of bivouac beside the piste, using your skis, poles, anorak, backpack – against which you can then lounge, soaking up the sun, like someone who has just been hard at it for three or four hours and needs a bit of a rest. If this is your speciality, it's worth getting hold of the sort of skis which provide the best support for lounging – nice and broad, comfortable binding for the small of the back, padded toe-piece to rest your head against.

As pointed out in *Piste Again*, when simply standing by the piste, it's important always to have something to keep you busy – which these days might be fiddling with your boot controls, waxes, or whatever – until there's a suitable moment to move off (i.e. when no-one is looking).

But you can also rely on stance alone – and the Survival Skier should spend some time working on this, and keeping up with all the new 'looking on' postures – a number of which depend on making good use of your *poles*. (Fortunately, they seem to be making them stouter these days and they are less likely to bend if they have to take your whole weight.)

For the more advanced Survival Skier, there's the one where you hoist yourself into a sitting position on your poles, supporting your legs by planting your skis vertically in the snow. You won't be able to hold this for too long, and it does need a bit of practice. But if you can sit there relaxed and beaming for a minute or so while your friends come whizzing and crashing past down the piste, you should be able to suggest a sort of effortless superiority.

For the Survival Skier who prefers something a little simpler, there's always the classic 'stand easy' position, one leg bent and forward of the other as you support yourself on your poles at around chest level. This works best if you look slightly pooped, as if just taking a breather before dashing on down. A variant of this is the more crouched position, sliding backwards and forwards on your skis and pushing on your poles as if getting ready to jump-start, and doing your best to look like the kind of skier who thinks nothing of skiing down the roofs of

off-piste huts and cottages. You might also try doing a few press ups on your ski poles from time to time; or jumping yourself around 180° on your poles (not as hard as it looks).

When it comes to actually moving off down the piste, the Survival Skier will usually traverse in a kind of easy zig-zag (see *Piste Again*). But here too your poles can come in very handy. One way of disguising the fact that the traverse is actually your standard method of skiing down is to aim on each traverse for some collapsed novice, and then offer your pole to help him or her up. Be careful though that they don't drag you down with them. It's always worth being solicitous to novices, by the way, thus adding to your coterie of admirers. When you see them later in the village, always stop to enquire: 'Did you manage to get down OK?' (Omit to mention that you *rode* down in the cable car.)

You can also make good use of lifts *going up*. (The Survival Skier, of course, will always pick the ones with the longest queues and spend a good deal of time at the bottom, *just to one side of the queue*, casually leaning on his sticks and chatting up the lift-man. It's a pity so many resorts are now introducing those little plastic cards.) When you do eventually go up in the chair, why not try sitting side saddle, or tangling your skis up in the bars. Done with the right sort of aplomb this can earn you more admiring glances than the piste-artists below you slaloming down between the pylons. If it's a double chair, of course, these sort of antics may not altogether be appreciated by your companion.

On a t-bar or poma, you can also jiggle about (this is even being encouraged in some French resorts – 'to get the feel of your skis'); and it's often a good wheeze to come off half-way, ducking off piste into some nearby forest. Pick your spot carefully though. You don't want to have to plough through too much wilderness to find yourself a congenial refuge – with the risk of ending up with more snow up your nose than there is on the piste. (If you are ever spotted buried in a drift, it's probably best to pretend that you were practising 'digging yourself a snowhole'.)

One problem though is that it's getting harder and harder to escape into some cosy mountain Hütte as more and more skiers are going off piste. It might, therefore, be worth pushing on off piste to the next village, finding a nice hotel with indoor pool and sunlounge to work on your tan, and then reappearing in your own resort at the end of the day to announce: 'Found this marvellous suntrap up in the wild on the other side of the mountain'. Lest any of your friends ask you to take them there, it may be worth adding 'Nearly got a nasty touch of frostbite on the way back though. Rubbed myself with snow. But could hardly get rid of it. Thought at one point the skin was frozen solid and I'd have to chip out some flesh. Lucky I had my ice-axe with me.' (One tip: get the taxi-driver who brings you up from the other village to drop you a hundred metres or so short of your resort, leaving you to shuffle in on your skis. Otherwise people might have a few doubts about your story.)

4 INSTRUCTION

'And everybody's going 'Shoosh, shoosh, shoosh. I feel the snow. I feel the cold. I feel the air.' . . . They all felt something. But I felt nothing – except the feeling that this bullshit was absurd.'

From the song 'Nothing', A Chorus Line

Even though increasingly skiers seem to be looking to state-of-the-art equipment to help them to achieve The Big Breakthrough, there are many who still think that ski-school can do something for them. Somehow, somewhere, many of us believe, there must be a Skilehrer, moniteur or maestro who will be able to bring forth all our latent skiing ability.

This belief has been fostered by the proliferation in recent years of new 'methods' of tuition – although there still don't seem to be many schools which teach the really useful skills; like how to keep your balance in the cafeteria in wet ski boots while carrying your lunchtray to your table; how to say 'help' while travelling downhill at 45 mph; or how to make a successful excursion to the loo while wearing salopettes or a one-piece.

These days, it's no longer just a toss-up between the classic Austrian, French, Italian and Swiss methods. In more and more resorts, you'll find competing ski schools – offering everything from the traditional methods to 'inner' or 'guru' skiing, not to mention mono lessons, powder classes, mogul clinics, racing schools, hot-dogging practice, ski voile and so on.

This was perhaps to be expected. The traditional 'bend ze knees' and 'one two three – after me' methods haven't really achieved dramatic results. (If people ski better now, it's probably not so much because of the tuition as of the technology and because skiers are now spending that much more time on the snow.)

This is hardly surprising really. No one who learned to ski as soon as he could walk (i.e. most instructors) actually *knows* how he does it. He just does it. And the reason he can do it is because he's been skiing since he could walk. And this experience of a lifetime on planks is not something you can very easily transmit in a week of ski-school. How can someone whose skis defy gravity understand the problems of people who can't even point their skis downhill? How can people who have one left foot and one right foot put themselves in the position of punters like us who as often as not take to the slopes with two left feet – and clay ones at that?

Nevertheless, the 'new' ski-schools *claim* to be able to do just this. And even

some Survival Skiers are being seduced by their ideas – despite the fact that deep down they know that all classes mean drill of one sort or another, and that good instruction is not really compatible with the Survival Skier's more individualistic approach.

But like other skiers they too continue to nurture the hope that the locals can pass on some of their knee-flashing magic – despite the fact that the skiers we most admire on the piste are often precisely the ones that our instructor will proceed to tell us are doing it all wrong. Instead of showing us how to emulate those elegant upright skiers who swoop serenely down the piste, they remain committed to putting us through the old thigh-squeezing squats as if they were training us up to be Cossacks.

It is, in fact, a favourite technique of instructors to pour scorn on the local hot-shots who dazzle us with their windshield wiper turns under the lifts:

'That boy should learn to *ski* before attempting that sort of thing'
'Now, if he'd just practice that without sticks (like you've been doing), he'd get the whole thing a lot cleaner'

At least, the instructor will tell his (somewhat sceptical) class, they can be content that they are doing it the *proper* way.

But what is the *proper* way? One year they're telling us to ski feet together — and next year it's feet apart. Remember the way they used to tell you to keep *all* your weight on your downhill ski? And what about that 'unweighting' that used to be all the rage, and all those hours we spent trying to work out the difference between 'upward' unweighting and 'downward' unweighting, religiously following our instructors' advice to practice every night on the bathroom scales.

Survival Skiers would be well advised not to get involved in these doctrinal controversies. Far better to let the 'experts' fight it out among themselves about what we *ought* to be doing and concentrate instead on trying to do what you do a bit better than you did. The fact is that you can be pretty sure that this year's orthodoxy will be next year's heterodoxy.

Nevertheless, many a Survival Skier will probably want to see what some of the new 'schools' and 'methods' have to offer. (There may — unlikely but possible — just be one that will work for you.) Here then is a guide to some of the options.

○ PSYCHOLOSKI ○

These are the new methods, like 'inner skiing', which seem to have most caught the imagination — tempting skiers with the notion that here maybe, just maybe, is a system that can unlock all that inner potential that we all feel we possess. They also appeal because they're said to be 'non-striving' learning theories — i.e. gain without pain. Just a question of listening to your own 'inner voice', 'letting the force be with you', and helping Self I to make contact with Self II.

In practice, though, as anyone who has ever watched an inner skiing class, let alone taken part in one, will know, it's actually jolly hard work: skiing without your sticks; skiing on one leg; 'skating' on the flat; pretending you're a gorilla on skis; trying to ski 'like the worst novice you ever saw'; skiing blindfold or with your eyes shut; playing egg and spoon races; passing balloons between your legs; imagining you're sitting on the lavatory (you will probably wish you were — skiing does tend to make you constipated, either as a result of nervous retention or by freezing up you inner tubes).

Whether all or any of this helps you to ski any better than good old 'bend ze

knees' is arguable. And anyone reared on the old methods may find it very hard to 'trust your body' (after all it's let you down often enough in the past). And is it all any more enjoyable – despite the fact that inner skiers are all encouraged to go around chanting: 'Smile – you are having fun'?

The problem for many Survival Skiers tends to be that if you haven't been sufficiently brainwashed by the silly exercises, your inner voice does tend to keep saying to you 'Now why on earth am I standing here behaving like such a bloody idiot?' Can they really be serious? I mean: 'stabbing at circles of snow to get rid of your troubles'; or 'saying thank you to moguls'; or 'talking to trees'. I ask you.

One might even ask if these methods are really all that new. After all, skiing Sloanes have for years at the shout of 'Dead Ant' been flopping onto their backs on the snow, wiggling their legs and arms in the air. And much good has it done *them*.

Still, some of the theoretical discussions can be quite interesting ('Does the snow know whether it's cold or not?'; or 'At what point does one turn finish and the next one begin?') And there are ways for the savvy Survival Skier to make it easier on himself: You can always spend a fair amount of time staring silently into space, and if quizzed, say simply 'I was meditating', or I was 'trying to feel At One with the mountain' (both of which responses will probably take you straight to the top of the class). Another nice thing is that you can always pull out for a couple of days saying: 'I think I should stay away a bit until my mental attitude is right.' There are some things to be said for a ski-school which specialises in 'understanding'.

○ 'MAESTRO' METHODS ○

This is not all that far removed from traditional methods of teaching. But there will be one new 'slant' – perhaps 'fluency' or 'flow', 'rhythm' or 'dynamic balance' or 'the pre-turn turn'. These 'systems' are usually promoted by a recently retired 'ski champion', who will claim that these were the secrets which took him to the top and which will revolutionise your skiing. Don't you believe it. In fact these methods would under normal circumstances not be taken much notice of – were it not for the reputation of the retired champion, desperately trying to cash in on his name before he is entirely forgotten. The 'maestro' will have got together a 'school' of disciples to promulgate the method which you may even find does help you to ski a bit better. The only problem is that when you go back to conventional ski-school, they'll tell you you're doing it all wrong.

○ SKI 'CLINICS' ○

These cater very much to drop-outs from other ski-schools and are often set up by a 'maestro' without the champion's reputation from one of the non-skiing

nations, like Britain. His line, therefore, tends to be: 'I may not be one of the greatest skiers of all time – but I am a great ski *teacher* and I understand the problems of people not born on the Alps.'

Like the 'maestro', he too will have his own variant on traditional methods which you will subsequently have to unlearn when you go back to conventional ski-school. You may also be confused by his insistence on not using the Standard Alpine terminology. Thus stem christie becomes 'plough swing', parallels become 'basic swing' and 'wedel' becomes 'short radius turns'. He will also have a lot of new terms of his own – like 'relaxed mode', 'stretched mode' etc.

What may appeal, though, is the opportunity that will be given to you to pour forth your tales of how you've been mistreated and abused by every other skiing instructor you've ever come across (and who hasn't?) His methods should, therefore, suit the more chauvinistic Survival Skier who enjoys being with an instructor who spends much of his time explaining how all the other nationalities on the slopes are doing it all wrong.

The problem is that your guru will require you to display total faith in his theories, as he expounds his original ideas and his conviction of the need to improve teaching skills *in the Alpine nations*. And if you show the slightest doubt, he can get rather tough on you, putting you through endless silly exercises and making you keep confessing to the rest of the class ('Now what were you doing wrong this time, Peter?') This, incidentally, he will probably call 'talking it through'.

○ SHORTCUT ○

Another new method where the gimmick is that it misses out a stage i.e. you go straight from snow-plough to parallel. But what, the Survival Skier might ask, do you fall back on? Some of us prefer a good old stem turn to using our bottoms.

○ MONO-SKIING ○

For anyone who already skis on two planks as if they were one, mono-skis shouldn't prove too much of a problem. It might even be easier – after all you've only got *one* board to worry about instead of two and, as the mono skischools will tell you: 'All you need is a basic sense of balance'.

Unfortunately, of course, this is precisely what most Survival Skiers lack, and when you fall off a mono – as you are going to do a lot at the start – climbing back on board ain't that easy. Even standing around (that Survival Skiing speciality) isn't that easy: any attempt to take a breather on a mono – on the piste anyway – is agony on the ankles (whether you're on the type where the

heels are locked together, or where they're slightly apart). You also tend to oversteer and find yourself paddling madly with your ski sticks to point yourself back down. And those sharp turns, flinging your whole body around, are not recommended if you suffer from a slipped disc. If you do catch an edge, of course, you're going to provide much more spectacular entertainment for onlookers than you would falling on two skis. You may just get your own back though – since, despite the restraining straps, runaway monos are not uncommon.

Monos, however, might have some appeal to the Survival Skier who has never absorbed anything about skiing on two planks – and so won't have to *un*learn anything. At least there aren't any tips to cross. And as we said earlier, you can make quite an impression – provided you can just about master the art of traversing and then disappear off-piste.

○ SNURFING ○

Once again, the propaganda is seductive – no hard boots (you can even wear your docksides), no poles to get in the way, no long skis to get crossed, and they're a lot quicker. (This last might perhaps not be quite such an appealing feature to the Survival Skier.)

It's promotors also claim that it's easier than skiing or mono-skiing. ('Just face sideways. You can pick up the basics in a couple of hours'), and that here, at last, is a type of skiing where 'anything goes'. (You, perhaps? Or some other part of your anatomy?) They do assure you, however, that it's impossible to break a leg snow-surfing – even though the bindings do *not* release. If you do take a tumble, by the way, do try to see that you end up facing up the slope in a kneeling position, not flopping *down* the slope on your bottom.

One advantage for the Survival Skier is that you can use *all* of the mountain (like monos, surfers are at their best *off*-piste) – so there is some scope for doing your thing out of sight i.e. chatting up the barmaid in some cosy mountain refuge.

Another advantage with both snurfers and monos is that liftmen often refuse to let you go up – thus providing the Survival Skier with another excuse for *not* performing. (You'll have to pretend, of course, that you've never heard of those short surfboards which clip onto your skis.)

○ SKI EVOLUTIF ○

No longer all that new and a teaching method that hasn't spread much beyond France. A sort of variant on the oldfashioned system when you *started out* on very long skis and then changed to shorter ones when you couldn't get the hang of it.

Totally Piste

The problem is that once you've got the hang of a comfortable length of mini-ski, you've then got to change to another. It can also come a bit expensive. (There are some who claim it was probably invented by a Frenchman who manufactured baby skis only to find that business was dropping since two year olds these days seem to move straight on to two metre planks.)

Not really a thing for the Survival Skier since the idea is supposed to be to teach you how to ski from scratch – and the Survival Skier should be a bit above this.

○ HANG-GLIDING ○

Hang-gliding on skis, usually with an instructor. (You don't *have* to have someone with you, but the Survival Skier may prefer to.) Actually not as hard as it looks. You only need to be able to ski well enough to take off and land (preferably upright).

Not a bad bet for the reputation-building Survival Skier – if he can afford the cost. (If you do go up, it's worth trying to ensure that you can only be seen by your skiing chums from quite a distance. That way they might not notice the instructor up there with you, whose presence would, of course, detract a bit from your image as 'Icarus on skis'.)

Other variants are delta-skiing and paragliding. But the Survival Skier should be careful here – the idea is to perform *without* an instructor.

○ SKI SAILING ○

As with snurfing, could be one for the Survival Skier who knows how to windsurf. The way these boards are sailed is not dissimilar; and you can 'carve', jump, slalom (uphill too) or even 'tack' and 'jibe' up the piste – standing side-on in your après-ski boots. If you'd rather stick with your usual skis, you can also get a sailboard rig mounted onto a crossbar attached to your skis.

As with monos and other 'new way' inventions, there is the big advantage for the Survival Skier that lift operators don't like them – even when you go up on another pair of mini-skis carrying your rig. You won't be very popular either with other people in the queue – though if you swing your sail crossways it can be a good way of preventing queue jumpers.

Of course, you can try getting uphill with one of those ski-parachutes, using the wind to blow you up. This can make quite an impressive sight – until the wind drops and you collapse downhill with all your kit and caboodle (also quite an impressive sight but one that will do rather less for the Survival Skier's reputation).

For the less ambitious Survival Skier, who is more attached to the rig than to the experience of sailing it, there is one very handy cop-out. The fact is you really need a clear piste for this sort of thing (and where do you find a clear piste these

28

days?) So you can just hang around at the bottom, looking mournful and amusing yourself with a bit of sail-tweaking.

◯ THE UNDERGROUND SCHOOL ◯

One way to minimise your 'tuition' costs. These are schools run by various types of ski bum (often Australian or American) who get their clients by undercutting the recognised schools. Since, however they are not strictly 'legit', the class will tend to have to assemble behind some chalet at the edge of the village (probably where your instructor's chalet bird/girlfriend works) and then head straight into the powder. The problem is that these boys often don't seem to have heard of the 'fear factor'. They just love to ski and that's what you may find yourself doing a bit too much of the time. Any dashes across the piste will probably be over some little frequented stretch of concrete washboard so that you're not spotted by the official skischool. So do make sure you have no loose fillings in your teeth. However, if a Survival Skier can survive a spine-crunching afternoon with him, it would at least mean you could probably ski anything.

◯ SPEED SKIING ◯

This used to be restricted to the 'Kilometro Lanciato' boys. But it's now being offered (though not quite a kilometre's worth) at some of the modern French resorts. Not all that hard actually – if you've got the nerve. Just point your skis downhill and go. With any luck a fall will slow you down sooner rather than later. If later, then you may just turn out to be one of the few Survival Skiers that didn't survive. Still, no guts, no glory.

◯ SLALOM ◯

There are schools for this too these days. Fortunately the new World Cup rules *seem* to indicate that the aim is to knock down all the spring-loaded poles with your shoulders as you go down. Might just, therefore, suit the Survival Skier who had been doing it this way – admittedly with the *whole* of his body – long before they ever changed the rules.

◯ OFF-PISTE SKIING/POWDER ◯

Has become popular with skiers who feel they are a bit above conventional instruction and that 'real men' no longer ski on the piste. Also a lot of people don't want to be taught anymore and are looking for more of an 'off-piste guide'. 'Powder has come to the people.'

Quite why it has become so popular is hard to say since skiing through powder usually feels more like skiing through polyfilla. It may just be all those glorious looking pictures of people (who know how to do it) skiing through the Bugaboos. But at least it will cure you of the habit of looking at your skis since you won't be able to see them.

In fact a good deal of time will be spent reassembling yourself after 'headplants', wiping the snow out of your goggles and trying to get your skis back on with ice-cold fingers after extracting them from under a tree root or a wire fence. There will also be a lot of searching for lost equipment in the snow — and so need not be too bad for the Survival Skier who enjoys a breather (provided he doesn't volunteer to help with the digging).

As mentioned earlier though, the Survival Skier might do just as well for himself by standing at the edge of the piste making a display of poking at the powder to check for consistency; and then positioning himself at the bottom of a beautiful set of snaking powder tracks, and looking back up at them as if they were his own handiwork (or rather footwork). 'Bit of a climb to get up there', he could say to anyone chancing to pass, 'but worth every minute for that run down'.

○ HELI-SKIING ○

If you are going to go into the powder, why not go the whole hog. Actually there are quite a number of reasons why not — avalanches, whiteouts, and the prospect of being buried in the powder for ever if you end up in one of those 3-metre tree holes.

If, however, you survive, it does mean you'll probably never have to ski off-piste again. 'Once you've heli-skied, nothing else could ever do', you can tell them, and then proceed to reminisce about the day you skied 40,000 vertical feet before lunch.

Some Survival Skiers, however, have been known to have second thoughts when they actually get up there. If this turns out to be your case, your best bet might perhaps be to set off an avalanche when no-one is looking, or to take your high altitude radio with you and claim you've just heard about a storm blowing up. This might just persuade the rest to take the next helicopter back down — that way it wouldn't look as if you were the *only* one chickening out.

○ POWDER

The day you decide to go off-piste is the day everyone decides to go off-piste

Going off-piste is usually more for the instructor's sake than yours

Whatever you are doing wrong, the instructor will tell you to lean forward more or to sit back more

If you carry your skis 'properly' over your shoulder when you approach the helicopter, the main rotor may see to it that you return home with a very short pair of skis

The ski that gets lost in the powder will be found further away than anyone thought — if it is found at all

The deeper the powder, the more likely you are to have forgotten to zip up one or more of your pockets

The line you took through the trees is never the line you intended to take through the trees

If you head for a slope of virgin powder in order to make the first wiggle in the snow, someone will get there before you

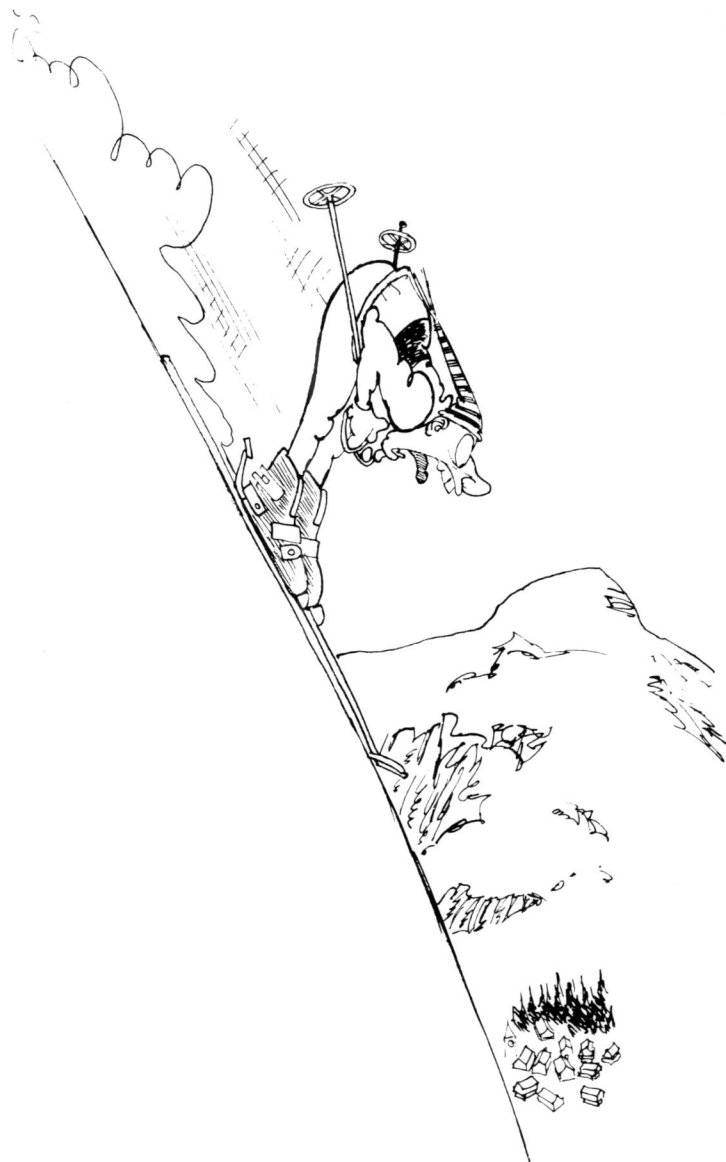

○ COULOIR SKIING – SKI EXTREME – SKI ESPACE – APOCALYPSE SKIING – SKI SAUVAGE ○

A nice simple sort of skiing – there are basically just two options: you will either

live to tell the tale, or you will die. Perhaps worth considering for the Survival Skier with big *cojones* who enjoys a game of Russian roulette with his Glühwein.

The advantage is that if you do come through – and someone gets a picture of you on your way down (make sure he shoots it at about 1/2000th of a second at least) – you may never have to ski again. (You may, of course, never be *able* to.) You will be able to rest on your laurels forever after – occasionally rolling up at the restaurant with your pair of special couloir skis that Sylvan Saudan helped you to design.

It might be easier though to get your photographer friend to photograph you on these skis standing on a jagged, but level, piece of terrain, with a look of terror on your face, doing your own version of Saudan's 'hop turn'. You then get the picture mounted *sideways*, so that it looks as if you're hurtling *down* a couloir. If any other skiers ask you why you're not seen on the slopes too much these days, all you need to do is take the picture out of your wallet, say that's really the only kind of skiing for you but that you've rather lost your nerve since you took that tumble last year. They should understand.

○ **MOGUL SKIING** ○

An excursion to Bump City to do battle with the Munch Monsters which probably won't appeal to most Survival Skiers. In any event, surely the technology should soon be getting to a point where they'll be able to eliminate bumps altogether. So there doesn't seem to be much point in learning how to ski them. Anyway, confusion still seems to rage about whether to ski *through* the bumps, *over* the bumps or *around* the bumps.

○ **SKI VOILE** ○

This is skiing with round glass-fibre wings attached to your arms or to your poles to help you 'fly through the air'. Despite assurances about 'high speed stability' and 'air-flap' braking, many Survival Skiers may find they are happy enough with the more modest flights they take on the piste when they come over an unexpected bump.

○ **SKI ARTISTIQUE** ○

Ballet, moguls, aerials. A great many of these flips, are not unlike the positions many Survival Skiers will have found themselves in at one time or another – whether it be a Spreadeagle, or Royal Christie or belly flop (you are often expected to practise in a wet-suit in a swimming pool).

No reason, though, why the Survival Skier shouldn't pretend to be a bit of an Evel Knievel on skis – adding, however, that he prefers to do his own thing: 'I just don't like the way hot-dogging has become codified these days. These people are acrobats, not skiers, and ought to be kept inside a circus'.

○ **VIDEO** ○

Used by all sorts of classes these days. The only advantage is that you will spend a lot of time sitting around – preferably inside – 'talking about it'. Picking out the faults that everybody else is making is actually quite fun. But when it gets to your own, it can be a bit of a blow to your skiing ego. (To quote '*Piste Again*': 'No-one skis like he thinks he skis'.)

○ SCHOOL

It is easier to imitate bad skiers than good skiers

No-one who can really ski well – like the local hot-shots – ever learned in ski school

The more people in the class, the less time you will spend skiing, and the less attention will be paid to the instructor

There are always more people in the class than you were led to expect

In any ski class between one third and one half of the pupils will assume that they are the best in the class

At some point in the week at least one skier in the class will be advised by the instructor to undo the top clip of his boots

The part of your body you actually lean into the turn is not the part of your body you thought you were leaning into the turn

---

5 SELECTING YOUR INSTRUCTOR

'Do you want us to fall over?'

Prince Charles

As you may have gathered from the previous chapter, many of the new methods may just promise a bit more than they actually deliver. And some Survival Skiers have come to the conclusion that they are no worse off sticking to the traditional methods.

Here, too, though, there have been some useful recent developments. There is, for instance, a trend now for ski schools to display on their notice boards photographs of all their instructors, with a brief indication of their specialities. Thus you do have more of an opportunity to select your instructor and to pick someone who suits your particular style.

Not that you will necessarily learn a lot from the picture. The older instructors often provide photos of themselves taken a couple of decades previously. And whatever the photo may look like, the chances are that in the flesh your instructor will tend to be the archetypal unshaven garlic-scented bandy-legged weatherbeaten hunchback with a cigarette dangling out of the corner of his mouth; or, it it's a woman, a sort of Alpine Amazon. So much for the bronzed Killy lookalikes of legend. This can actually make it all the more frustrating: if this bow-legged simian can do it, surely a beautiful talented person like you should be able to make a better fist of it.

In fact the descriptions under the photos often can be of more help if you can interpret them properly. 'Has taught at resorts all over the Alps' probably means he hasn't been able to hold down a job in any of them. 'Can instruct in English' as likely as not means he doesn't speak English. Whatever his or her recommendations, however, it's probably better not to expect too much of your instructor. After all, any job where you're unemployed half of the year, paid a minimum wage, and work in freezing conditions is going to produce some fairly frustrated individuals – particularly towards the end of the season.

True, he or she may just *love* skiing – but skiing with a bunch of clowns like you? (There's *not* a lot of competition among ski instructors to take the least competent classes.) Perhaps the most candid appraisal you will get from your ski instructor is that look when he first claps eyes on his new class, and which often amounts to: 'Here we go again. Another prize set of duffers. Don't I get

35

'em.' They do say an instructor can tell how someone skis just by watching them ride up the t-bar.

But even though they are probably better at assessing you, than you are at assessing them, it pays for the Survival Skier also to be able to suss out his potential mentors at an early stage. The following profiles may help to give you a clearer idea of what to look for.

○ **THE DRILL SERGEANT** ○

Believes in teaching skiing by numbers, putting you through endless agonising knee-jerk exercises, playing silly games (like jumbling up everybody's skis in a pile and getting you to fetch them), and generally getting you to do things that are even more difficult than skiing. 'Now I want you to jump from big toe to big toe holding your sticks in the air.' This will provide some light relief for other classes who will enjoy watching him put you through your paces. They'll always know where to find you – your instructor's 'fog horn' voice can be heard all over the mountain.

○ THE CONFUSER ○

Specialises in telling you too much, all at once: 'Get your weight forward — now *use* your pole — and *watch* where you're going — don't forget to look for your *hands*.' In the unlikely event that you do manage to do all these things, he still won't be satisfied: 'And which way were you supposed to be facing — do I have to spell everything out?'

○ THE FLATTERER ○

Knows that the ego of the recreational skier is a fragile thing and that you'll think the more of his instruction if he can persuade you that you are better than you really are: 'You certainly wear your skis well'. This is not an altogether misguided theory since in skiing, confidence is all. Might, therefore, suit the Survival Skier who wants reassurance that he can do no wrong. Even when you just manage to stay upright after a nasty bump, arms akimbo and one leg in the air, he'll offer something like: 'Nice piece of recovery skiing that.'

○ THE TRICKSTER ○

The sort who makes sure he stays one up on his class by never letting the class settle down to *their* pace. There will be some nice easy skiing; then without a word of warning he'll be getting you all to do little jumps or leading you straight into a field of moguls the size of haystacks, or down The Big One. He also always seems to be skiing that *bit* too fast, or more likely that *bit* too slowly for a particular piece of piste. In this case the Survival Skier might be better advised to just do his own thing and ski on past him. ('See you at the bottom, boss.')

○ THE GLOATER ○

Has discovered that the best way to boost his class's ego (and the class's faith in *his* teaching ability) is to spend a good deal of time gloating at even worse classes — or perhaps better classes just as they are in the process of attempting some 'Ski That?' precipice. Your class can then stand there and watch them all fall down, and then ski off down an easier route, noses in the air, with your morale much boosted. A type of instructor who might well suit the Survival Skier.

○ THE OBSCURE ○

Not a bad choice for the Survival Skier as you can always pretend (with some justification) that you don't understand what he says: 'So *that's* what you wanted

me to do'. Not that he will give up easily. And he can get quite menacing if you keep on failing to get his drift: 'You no understand English?' Make sure you don't let him get away with this and reply clearly: 'No, *you* don't understand English'. Unintelligibility is actually quite a common failing among ski instructors. Try learning in Scotland, for instance; or with one of those Brits who has read all those ski manuals and jabbers away at you all the time in arcane Skinglish.

○ THE SALESMAN ○

Has a little thing going with his cousin who owns a ski shop. Will, therefore, spend most of his time trying to persuade each member of the class (and they very often don't need much persuading) that they would ski much better if they were on a different type of skis. Fortunately, *he* knows somewhere where you can get a good discount, and he will be only too happy to help you to select a new pair one evening.

○ THE REALIST ○

Makes no attempt to conceal his belief (probably well-founded) that most of you in his class are probably never going to make it: 'You *may* get the hang of it – in about ten years time.' (Ha! Ha!) Better this, though, than the type who believes it's possible for even *you* to learn to ski, and keeps on promising an imminent breakthrough. (You are bound to disappoint him – and yourself.)

○ THE RE-EDUCATOR ○

Spends most of his time explaining to you that everything you've learnt everywhere else is wrong. So now it's his sorry lot to try to correct all those sloppy habits you've picked up in Italy or Andorra or somewhere. (For an Austrian or a Swiss this can explain everything – even *your* performance on planks.) The problem is that he usually insists on going right back to basics: 'Now we must learn again the first lesson – falling down. Tomorrow we learn the second lesson – getting up.' Not the sort of instructor the Survival Skier would be looking for.

○ THE ROMEO ○

May not exactly be the hyper-smooth demi-god that ski instructors are popularly imagined to be. But that won't stop him trying. He'll take every opportunity to massage the thighs of his female charges as if they were downhill racers being

prepared for the 'off'. With these protégés he will tend not so much to demonstrate positions as to physically 'arrange' their bodies into the right stance. The advantage is that he'll probably leave the rest of you pretty much alone. If he does start pushing you around, though, it may not be a bad idea to 'plant' one of the little goers in your class on him — so that the next day she can criticise *his* performance (under the duvet).

○ THE FAVOURITISER ○

Similar type. Picks out one or two favourites in the class on the first day — often including the most attractive female — and devotes all his attention to them. They are the ones who get to ski behind him all the time, go up on the lift with him, and receive the benefit of most of his advice. May suit the Survival Skier who prefers to be left to his own devices by the instructor.

○ THE THEORETICIAN ○

Believes theory is as important as practice, and will spend more time talking

39

than skiing. Not a bad bet, therefore, for the Survival Skiier who enjoys talking technicalities, and brushing up his ski-speak. The problem is that all these explanations about what makes a ski turn (interesting though they may be) won't necessarily make *you* any better at turning on skis. And you'll also find, when you do perform, that all those complicated instructions he calls out to you bear very little relation (unfortunately) to what you're actually doing, i.e. just trying to stay upright on your skis as you bounce through a mogul field.

○ THE BOOZER ○

Often an oldtimer with a paunch and a red nose, who believes it's important to 'bend ze elbow' as much as to 'bend ze knees'. Much of your time, therefore, will be spent adjourning to hostelries near the slopes and sitting around to 'discuss your problems'. On the slope too, he'll probably be able to supply the class with some fortifying firewater and other goodies from his backpack – just to help you 'relax'. For obvious reasons, not a bad bet for the Survival Skier. And if you ensure that you too always have a couple of hip-flasks to pass around, you'll probably find yourself top of his class.

○ THE SPEED-MERCHANT ○

The one with the extra-long 'demo' skis. Often an ex-downhiller who never made it into the big league. He will just keep disappearing off the end of the world, and expect the class to follow. No sooner will they catch up with him, skis flapping in their faces, teeth chattering in time to their skis, than he'll be off again: 'Last one down buys the drinks.' An afternoon with him can thus come a bit expensive for the Survival Skier who likes to hang back a bit.

○ THE TOUGHIE ○

The instructor who is always detailed to take the class where they've put all the 'Type-T' personalities – the daredevils, doers and delinquents. His first priority, therefore, will be to clip their wings a bit – leading them up and down the Abbatoir Piste at double time and off the sort of precipices where your suntan immediately fades when you get to the edge. Probably, therefore, not one for the Survival Skier – though there is a certain aura attached to being a member of the 'Suicide Squad'.

○ **THE SONGBIRD** ○

Has a bit of a voice, or can yodel, and enjoys displaying these gifts as he leads his troupe down the piste. All very jolly. The trouble is that this will just draw attention to your class; and that's the last thing the Survival Skier wants. Even worse are the ones who see their class as a potential chorus: learning to ski is hard enough – without having to learn the words of 'La Montanara' at the same time.

○ **THE REGRADER** ○

The instructor who is never content to stick with the class-members he has been allotted, and is, therefore, constantly looking to promote some and to demote others. ('OK. If you too stupid, down to next class.') In fact, this may just be a subtle way of encouraging the weaker brethren to shape up: just imagine! The shame, the ignominy of having to join the class that you've been spending your time looking down your nose at – and most of whom you will now probably discover are better than you are.

○ **THE ENGINEER** ○

More of a do-it-yourself-man than a skier. Gets much more pleasure from adjusting all your equipment than he does from teaching you how to ski, and will have a rucksack full of tools to tune up your bindings and your skis. Not that this will make any more difference to your skiing than instruction would. A good choice, perhaps, for the Survival Skier who is not looking to put in too much mileage. If necessary, you can always get him to stop to 'check the adjustment' of one of your spoilers, or fiddle around with some other part of your equipment.

○ RUNS

One man's schuss is another man's precipice

If you have one good run, don't expect to have a second

You will have more bad runs than good ones

You are more likely to fall if you look up at the chair-lift

Only the perfect skier never looks up at the chair-lift

The colour of a run is never the way you would rate it

A black run in Italy is not the same as a black run in France or a black run in Austria

It's easier to get onto a black run than off one

---

6 TRAINING YOUR TUTOR

**'That's enough for today.
Let's all go back to the restaurant.'**

John Lennon, after his first ten minutes skiing in St. Moritz.

Now, some of these types we've mentioned may seem a bit fearsome – but perhaps not as much as they once would have done. For another positive recent development is that instruction is increasingly being seen as a *two-way process*, and not simply as a case of 'Achtung, bereit, los' or 'follow-my-leader'.

This means that the skilled Survival Skier should be able to see to it – and earn the respect and gratitude of his classmates into the bargain – that your instructor also comes in for a bit of training. No harm at all in making him go through his routines a few times, then shaking your head and getting him to try them again. You could also try placing someone directly behind him to ski on his heels, and so bring him crashing down – which won't be the best thing for his image – though it wasn't exactly his fault.

With this sort of approach you should be able to get your instructor *in tune with you* by the end of the week, if not before: stopping when *you* want to; doing the exercises *you* prefer; sticking to the pistes that *you* choose (declining his suggestions that you go off piste); lunching late or early as *you* decide (and make sure *he* is back on time – *you* can be late, but *he* can't). Make it clear from the start that he is your hired hand and that he'd better be civil or you will just have to find someone else.

Perhaps the most effective training technique to employ is the one which many instructors themselves have been using for years on their pupils – first destroying the class's confidence, and then spending a week rebuilding it. It can be easier to turn the tables on your instructor than you may think. Some of these types – even though they may look indestructible – have surprisingly fragile egos. And their confidence can often be as easily shattered as yours. A few well-chosen remarks on that first morning may be all that you need:

> 'How long have you been teaching exactly?' (Perhaps to a younger instructor.)
> 'So that's how they're teaching Christie's now, is it?'
> 'Have you ever taught *English* people before?'
> 'How dare you address my friend like that – it looked like a perfectly good turn to me.'

43

'How do you expect us to do it, if you can't do it right?'
'Try again old son. Walk up here and see if you can get it right this time.'
'Would you mind demonstrating that again?'
'Get your hands off me' (if he tries to rearrange your limbs into the correct position).

You could also try forgetting his name from time to time: 'Now look here. What's your name again? . . .'

And don't neglect the effect of the odd remark made to your classmates, which he will also be able to overhear: 'The only reason he does those turns better than us you know, is those special skis of his.' (If he offers to swap, it may be wiser to decline the offer. This might prove a bit embarrassing for you.) Or perhaps: 'We learnt more in three hours in Pistendorf last year than we have in the last three days with this chap.'

Another good idea is to mug up a bit of ski jargon and to ask him questions he can't answer. It pays to be knowledgeable about instruction – especially with the younger type of instructor. Make it very clear that you've had more instructors than he has had classes. Then, when he elaborately demonstrates a turn, whisper loudly to your classmates behind your hands: 'You know I really do think he's the best skier in the class' or 'Well that's certainly not what the last instructor told us.' Take every opportunity to enter into a discussion, contradicting him and arguing. If nothing else, this will at least give the class a chance to take a bit of a breather – which may be much needed if he's the type that sees to it that your class always has priority on ski lifts.

Another way to slow down the pace if your instructor's English isn't too hot is to get the class to keep scratching their heads and look puzzled and then try to interpret what he has said for one another's benefit. This, of course, can be great fun for the 'interpreters' who can then become surrogate instructors with the chance to try out some of their own theories. Skiing, of course, does tend to bring out the instructor in all of us.

Or, if your tutor has a habit of launching into particularly boring monologues, just clamp on your Walkman and look bored. If he takes exception to this, say: 'I was just listening to an instructional tape – to try to pick up a few useful tips.' You might also threaten to change class. Many instructors are quite sensitive on this score. They don't mind demoting people, but don't like their pupils to demote themselves, in case it reflects badly on them.

Now all this may sound a bit cruel. And, as we've said, instructors can be delicate souls – quite sensitive to how much their group likes them. (Nor do they want word to get back to the other instructors that they are unpopular, or that they can't speak English as they claimed when they got the job.) Many instructors also do want to be obliging, and, if encouraged, will be happy to keep

trotting out the ski stories at the café so that you don't have to go back to the slopes too soon. Nor are many of them too bothered if your skiing is not up to much. Some don't even like you to make too much progress. After all, they do like to feel needed.

In fact the best way to boost both your ego and his is to start the week pretending to be a prize duffer – or rather more of a prize duffer than you usually are. You can then proceed to make a dramatic improvement during the course of the week, earning yourself constant praise and also making him feel good about his instructional skills.

The truth is that a lot of instructors need reassurance every bit as much as their pupils – not, however, that they can *ski*, but that they can *instruct*. So once you've got him well-drilled, no reason not to start saying a few nice things about his instruction. He, in turn, may start saying nice things about your skiing. All in all, just the sort of 'two-way process' that modern instruction is supposed to be about.

7 GEAR

**'The first person to arrive in Mürren (in the twenties)
with a zip on his jacket was a fascinating sensation;
he got so fed up with people pulling the zip up and down
that in the end he fitted a padlock to its top.'**

Peter Lunn

When it comes to hardware, the rule is much the same as for softwear – the Survival Skier should have *as much of it as possible*. Some of it may even help. *Piste Again*, of course, did recommend sticking to tried and tested equipment – say hickory skis and bamboo poles – and maintaining a healthy scepticism about some of the more new-fangled inventions. But the fact is that people do now ski much better than they used to (a bit too well in fact for the Survival Skier who doesn't like to be shown up) and this just may have something to do with modern technology and wonder-materials like Kevlar and carbon fibre.

Also, as we've said, most of the chat around the slopes will be about skiing and equipment, even amongst the piste poseurs – so you can feel a bit left out if you're not bang up to date. So do be knowledgeable about the latest techniques and equipment – particularly the bits and pieces which *you* have acquired.

Don't worry about getting out of your depth. The Survival Skier, like everyone else, should go for the state-of-the-art stuff. Don't worry that it may be too good for you. No ski gear was ever designed for the mediocre skier. He or she does not exist. So, as with clothing, the Survival Skier should 'go for it' – provided he can afford the sort of equipment that ought really to be kept in a bank vault.

Top of the range gear may even add a little something to your performance. With any luck, in fact, it shouldn't be too long before the manufacturers really start living up to their claims, and the skiing itself is actually done for you. Computers at the foot of the slope and in your boots will process all the data about snow-coefficients, windspeed and so on, to help you to decide which ski to wear; and once you're skiing they will 'read' the snow for you, transmitting all the right messages to your laser-guided skis, and to your poles and to your body, which will be cocooned in a totally integrated solar-energised air-flow system.

Unfortunately, however, we're not quite there yet. The Survival Skier still has to do quite a lot for himself – though you'd never realise it from flipping through some of the brochures and ski mags. They all make it sound as if the equipment already needs a minimum of assistance from you. But many of their claims and counterclaims are actually quite confusing. To help you get all of this into perspective, therefore, let's have a closer look at what's currently available.

○ **BOOTS** ○

In the last few years boots seem to have superseded skis as *the* focus of interest. And in most lift queues, you'll find that far less time is spent looking at each other's clothes and skis than in examining the controls on one another's shin-bangers. (One recently introduced model in fact has no less than *nine* fit and performance controls — a sort of plastic box decorated with knobs, dials, ratchets and levers.)

Not that this means that beginners are any the less likely to put their boots on the wrong way round. Nor that your ankles and shins will get off any more lightly than they used to. You stand as good a chance as ever of getting an attack of 'the boots' — your feet imprisoned in those great triangular blocks, calves bent forward at an unnatural angle, and being rubbed up the wrong way in at least three separate places.

Now, that isn't the theory, mind. The idea of all these controls, with everything adjustable, is that you get a *perfect* fit, geared exactly to *your* type of skiing. The

fact is, though, that there are so many fine-tuning possibilities that you'll *never* get your boots set up-right – despite the 600-page instruction manual and the half-day course they gave you in the shop about how to 'drive' the boot and how to set it up to compensate for your hammer toes, fallen arches and knock-knees (all based on a diagnostic computer read-out of your 'pressure emphasis' and other personal characteristics).

One advantage of this for the Survival Skier is that you can spend a great deal of time on the slope fiddling with the controls on your boots, as you adjust for cant, flex and forward-lean. All quite an advance on just playing with your clips. The pity is that you still have to *bend down* to do it. How long are we going to have to wait for the manufacturers to come up with a remote-control box conveniently built into your anorak?

Needless to say, this sort of activity can also take up a fair amount of your *après*-ski time – recharging the boots, adjusting the central heating system, and checking that the avalanche locaters are working OK, or the piste-reading sensors on the toe-piece, or those reflectors at the back for night-time skiing. Still, this is one way of keeping away from the disco action – though it won't necessarily be much more peaceful, with all those flashing lights on your boots and on your 'boot charging unit'.

One last tip. Difficult as it may be to walk back to the chalet in your boots, on no account should you use those 'boot walkers' that clamp on to the bottom. This will mean that your lack of 'bootmanship' will be revealed to all who will see that you can't even set the flex adjuster to 'walk' position so that they move easily in the forward plane.

○ SKIS ○

The paradox about skis is that we all now buy our own on the basis that this will work out cheaper than renting over a period of three or four years, and we then proceed to invest in a new pair each season. The Survival Skier shouldn't worry about this too much, however, since, as we've seen, he or she needs as many pairs of skis as he can afford – piste skis, off-piste skis, hard skis, soft skis, slalom skis, downhill skis, as well as various types of novelty ski – so that he can spend a good deal of time chopping and changing to suit the conditions. To paraphrase the Duchess of Windsor: 'No woman can ever be too rich, too thin or have too many pairs of skis'.

As a general rule, the Survival Skier should be seen with the *longest possible* skis. And this indeed is the trend. Compacts have been succeeded by mids, and then by 'clipped' full length. (So much, incidentally, for the theory we were all led to believe, that it was compact skis which caused moguls: compact skis are long gone, but there is still no shortage of bumps on the piste.) Avoid those 'boutique'

skis, by the way. They may have a certain 'limited edition' snob appeal and be easier to ski on, but they'll do a good deal less for your reputation than your detuned racers.

Even if you aren't very tall, there's no reason (except possibly lack of skiing ability) that you shouldn't have long skis. How else are you going to be able to hold your head up as you wait for the cable car? So make sure everyone else in the queue is looking *up* at your ski tips. No matter that your instructor will be entirely contemptuous when he sees this. After all, it's not him you're trying to impress. One answer to this problem might just be those adjustable-length skis. (It might be worth noting that Lego have now started making ski equipment!)

The other important thing is to 'know your skis'. You've got to be as ready as anyone to hold forth on the merits of laminated carbon-fibre or assymetrical edges or vibration-dampening modules or whatever. This should pose no real problems — just read carefully the manufacturers' blind-them-with-rubbish puffs. (Have you ever come across a ski without a 'unique construction'?)

But do try not to fall too much in love with your skis. There are people who would happily take their skis to bed with them — and may even do so. (There are always people sneaking down to the ski-room at night and then back up the stairs.) Thus it can be a bit disheartening when your pride and joys are irreverently bunged into the back of the bus or the train with all the others. The Survival Skier, however, should *not* be the type who puts transparent film on his skis to stop his customised graphics from getting scratched; or has his name studded in diamonds on his custom-made sliders, or his own silk-screen design printed on. He knows that disposability is the name of the game. So don't bother with one of those burglar-alarm attachments.

Even though the Survival Skier should be well versed in the manufacturer's claims, he should also display a certain scepticism: he's not blind to the tendency of Kevlar to 'delaminate sideways'; or to how the effects of torque and sidecut often can cancel each other out. Not that this will prevent him from ensuring that he has all the new rubber attachments on his ski tips, the latest design in spoilers and air flow systems, and assorted knobs and counterweights to dampen those spine-crunching vibrations. He knows, though, that sooner rather than later the hole in the tip will have become as redundant as the parablack. (Whatever happened to those things, by the way? Why don't we need them anymore? People don't seem to be crossing their ski tips any less than they used to. Perhaps there just wasn't any room for both them and the mileage-gauge we'll all soon have on the front.)

The Survival Skier, however, shouldn't just leave it to the manufacturers to make all the improvements. He should be seen constantly peering down the barrels and 'air channels' of his skis, tuning up his edges, dulling the ski tips, rounding off or sharpening up the tails (split or otherwise), adjusting the length of his powder retaining straps, drilling holes in his boards and moving the

bindings backwards and forwards, and painting yet another substance onto his black graphite bases.

Waxing, of course, is back in fashion now. So much for those 'thermal' skis. The Survival Skier thus has yet another good way of keeping himself busy beside the piste. It's worth bearing in mind that you can also wax *to travel more slowly*. It's just a pity that sprays have rather put an end to the ritual of brewing up your wax. (Some resorts even have piste-side drive-in 'waxoramas'.) There seem to be sprays for everything now – your skis, your boots, your bindings, your clothing, as well as for assorted parts of your body.

One type of 'innovation' that the Survival Skier would, however, do better to ignore are all those gadgets for carting your skis around – those shoulder straps, clips or 'ski-totes', or those little wheels for pushing your skis around on. Any skier worth his salt has a little groove in his shoulder for lodging his skis (or, in the case of the Survival Skier, perhaps a little foam pad inside his anorak instead). One thing you might find useful though is the ski-box or roof-boot for the top of the car. This can be rather handy for keeping all your equipment in. (You may need two or three.) And, at a pinch, they would do as a coffin if the unexpected happens and you end up going home as 'brown bread'.

○ **BINDINGS** ○

The fact that you are that much less likely to end up as 'brown bread' these days is in no small measure a consequence of binding technology having got so good (as well, of course, as developments in the techniques of Survival Skiing). Never mind that they are now starting to make them out of plastic and rubber – they do still seem to do the job.

So it always seems a bit thankless that we should just chuck our bindings away and replace them whenever we get a new pair of skis (conveniently forgetting when we order our new skis to allow for new bindings in the final cost). But clearly, there's no reason why bindings should be an exception to the law of disposability which applies to all ski gear. And lest you should contemplate transferring your old bindings to your new skis, there are always some new refinements which would make this seem unwise. The binding-makers also seem to like to persuade us to keep on swapping brands, as they all take it in turns to lead the field – from Marker to Look to Salomon and back again to Look and Marker. The question is, with the introduction of micro-chip electronic bindings, will the Japanese also be willing to continue to alternate in this gentlemanly fashion?

This might perhaps be a subject for speculation for the Survival Skier, who should be as adept at talking about bindings as about anything else, holding forth on technicalities like 'equaliser' features and Twincam toes and the prospects of the plate-binding staging a comeback.

○ **POLES** ○

Sticks are also something that tend to be bought very much as an afterthought. Once you've got the skis, after months of agonising about the pros and cons of different types of plank, you are more than likely to settle for the first pair of poles the salesman hands you. (HIM: 'Here, try these for size.' YOU: 'They seem about right. I'll take them.')

But since some skiers weren't actually bothering to change their poles, the stickmakers have also been making annual alterations to ensure that we have to keep up to date. So we've gone from straps to sword-grips and back to straps. And every year there's a smaller basket on the end of your poles – whether they're the latest telescopic type, or elliptical ones, or wiggly 'corrective' angle poles, or designer 'wrist-assist' sticks in flashy colours with see-through handles.

One word of warning to the Survival Skier. You'd do better not to let yourself be tempted away from your Scott's by those poles that unfurl to make a sort of deckchair when clipped across your upended skis. This really does make you look like too much of an armchair skier. If you do want to lounge about on the piste like this (and no reason why you shouldn't), better stick to the 'old way' – propping yourself up against your skis, or perhaps using your bandanna or your poles to improvise a backrest between your skis.

○ GEAR

On any skiing holiday, you will spend as much time zipping up your clothes as zipping down the slopes

The more comfortable your boots while skiing, the less comfortable while walking

The likelihood of your boots hurting is substantially increased if that was the last pair in your size in the hire-shop, or if you rented them at home before coming out

No ski glove has yet been designed which keeps the tips of your fingers warm

At least one of your ski poles is always bent – either accidentally by you, or on purpose by the manufacturer

The fact that the binding released correctly when the assistant yanked it in the shop is no guarantee that it will release properly on snow

Just when you think you are going to get through the week with your new ski bases unscathed, you'll hit the rocks

○ **SOUND** ○

After 'Bend ze knees', probably the most common cry on the slopes these days is: 'Damn – my Walkman's bust again'. More and more skiers are now wired for sound; and for the Survival Skier this does have certain advantages. It means, for instance, that you can't actually *hear* when people are laughing at you. Nor will you have to listen to the crack when you snap a tendon or fracture a limb.

It also means that *you're* the one who gets to choose what you're listening to – not the chap who operates the loudspeakers on the pylons; or the person with the Walkman next to you in the queue. (The problem of 'sound overspill' is probably going to get worse rather than better with the introduction of 'sound jackets' – anoraks with inbuilt speakers and power boosters.)

There is one drawback though. As we know, the Survival Skier is someone who does enjoy giving others the benefit of his advice – it seems a pity that there are going to be fewer and fewer people around who are in a position to listen to him.

8 ON THE LEVEL

'Wait till I count my fingers. I may have lost one.'

'Scotty', in *The Thing from Another World*

Many an innocent Survival Skier has had the 'bright idea' of taking to cross-country for a couple of days as an easy and acceptable way of avoiding the agonies of Alpine skiing and the sheer cost of downhill high tech. It usually doesn't take long, however, for them to radically revise their opinions: shuffling along on skinny skis is not quite the doddle it looks.

Certainly, when you start out, it can seem like a distinct improvement on downhill. You can take your time and linger over breakfast – none of that early morning rush for the lift. You can then spend a while quietly in the 'salle de fartage' (the waxing room, incidentally, not the 'farting room' – though it is often characterised by its distinctive smell).

It's when you actually set out though and start moving that your ideas may begin to change a bit. The fact is that *you* are the one who has to move the skis – unlike downhillers, langlaufers don't rely on gravity. And after you've shuffled along a bit, it may suddenly begin to dawn exactly why those oldsters were taking their time at breakfast, and tucking supplies of food into their backpacks: the truth is that few activities on the planet burn up more calories per hour than this 'soft sport for oldies'.

It's then that you begin to see in a somewhat different light those genteel geriatrics shuffling along in kneesocks and knickerbockers. For one thing, a good many of them aren't quite that geriatric: they can't be – not at the speed they shuffle past you (who will more likely be going slowly nowhere while expending a great deal of energy). Nor, on careful examination, is a lot of the gear quite so old-fashioned. A fair number of skinny skiers will be clad in aerodynamic skintight fluorescent suits (though they often still stick to the long hat with the bobble). In many ways, in fact, loipegear is sexier than downhill gear – though you couldn't say the same about their tomato red faces once langlaufers get into their stride.

But whatever the pros and cons, there's no question that the popularity of cross-country has been growing dramatically – even among Brits. And the compleat Survival Skier, therefore, should also be able to hold his own in the ruts. Gone are the days when the Survival Skier could afford to look down on skinny skiers (jeering at them 'Telemark please' whenever he caught sight of one).

Fortunately, there are one or two techniques that can make things easier for the Survival Skier. As with 'avoidance skiing' on piste, for instance, there is always the option of ducking off the beaten-track and spending your time getting well-oiled in some little mountain hostelry. After all, traditionally, cross-country is supposed to be a sport for loners and nature lovers who enjoy getting out into the countryside, listening to the silence in the fir-glades, interrupted only by the birdsong, the babbling of brooks under the ice, browsing deer or the occasional nibbling winter hare. That's all part of the 'kick' of cross-country skiing.

If, instead, you stick to the loipes (which are fast becoming as crowded as the pistes) you'll find there isn't much scope for creative lingering. Practitioners tend to just charge along the marked rails, head down, in their tramlines to the next signpost. (If downhillers are said to go up and down like yo-yos, langlaufers could be said to go round and round in circles – and extremely *large* circles at

that.) Après-loipe tales told at the end of the day tend to concentrate overwhelmingly on how many kilometres you covered and how long it all took you.

So lying low in the woods in a sheltered spot is not such a bad idea. Then when the Survival Skier feels like a bit of company and wants to establish his presence, he can re-emerge from between the trees, duly fortified by the solid and liquid provisions in his knapsack, and park himself at one of those junctions where three or four loipes cross. There are often a fair number of people standing around at these places since it is never clear which arm of the sign is pointed in which direction, and any map will not agree with the signpost.

In fact, all loipe groups include a map-reader who will insist that though the sign may *look* clear, according to his map, there is a *better* way. (This is rarely the case – though I suppose it depends what you mean by better.)

Ideally, the Survival Skier should take up his position at the loipe junction at one of those moments when the coast is clear and there is no one else around. Then when people do appear, he can stand there looking puffed, loaded down by his well-stuffed pack (as if he's been on the trail for days) or perhaps towing a sled and offering, on the basis of *his* experience, advice on the best route to take.

Another ploy is to set out from your base on a lollipop-shaped loipe. You should be able to make it up the stick of the lollipop and a bit beyond – onto the start of the circuit. You can then turn around to head back (slowly), pretending to anyone you meet that you've actually been *right round* the circuit in the other direction.

On no account, however, should you actually try to complete the course. All loipes are actually longer than the direction indicators show and it will always be a good deal further than it looks on the map. Another rule to remember is that it's always shorter on the way out than it is on the way back – so beware of straying out too far. There's also no point in trying to select your route so that you have the wind with you in at least one direction. You can be absolutely sure that if the wind is against you on the way out, it also will be against you on the way back.

For the Survival Skier who really wants to cop out though, and enhance his reputation into the bargain, there's probably nothing to beat the 'early bird' routine. This involves arriving a bit late for breakfast, in a damp pair of kneesocks, with a bit of frosting in your hair, looking a bit pooped and sweaty. (A few physical jerks outside in the snow beforehand should see to this.) You then breeze in, looking flushed and pleased with yourself at having 'got in your twenty kilometres' before breakfast, and being generally hearty to all and sundry: 'Nothing like getting out there just when the birds are waking up'. That, of course, will be the last anyone sees of you on the loipes that day.

In fact, heartiness is one of the most important skills a langlaufer has to master. Cross-country skiers are for ever pronouncing 'Herrlich, nicht?' and wishing one another 'Viel Spass'. Such greetings are very much the thing when

you meet other langlaufers en route. However puffed they are, they'll offer at least a 'Guten Tag', to which (if they've got in first) you should reply: '*Schönen Guten Tag*' or '*Wunderschönen Guten Tag*'. It's all part of the cross-country philosophy that 'Langlaufers laugh longer' – as well as 'love longer' and 'live longer' (or so they say). The Survival Skier may well have his doubts about this latter claim. No statistics have yet been produced of how many cases of cardiac arrest occur on loipes each year. But all those little shrines dotted around the mountains would seem to indicate that it's a fair old number.

When the Survival Skier is out on a loipe and not skulking in the woods, he'll generally do best to stick to the well-trodden trails. But do stay well away from those smaller circular nursery-type loipes where everyone can watch everyone else going round. It can be a bit embarrassing to keep on being lapped by people who are either half or twice your age.

Out on a proper trail, it should be easier to cut a better figure. But do be careful not to give yourself away. You can show yourself up very easily by the way you handle yourself on the track. The pros, for instance, swop ruts without thinking twice about it; the amateurs tend to hang onto their ruts no matter what. In some respects, though, it does pay to be the weaker skier. This should mean you are left to plod along in the well-trodden tramlines, leaving it to the stronger skier to ski wide – perhaps even having to make some new tracks.

At times, of course, there will be some joker coming straight at you in *the opposite direction* in your right-hand track (probably another downhiller, 'giving it a go'), and turning the whole thing into a game of 'chicken'. This is when you should loudly voice your contempt for the sort of people they are now letting onto the loipes and offer a few lessons in the highway code – making the point clear with the tip of your pole if necessary

Another type to beware of are the overtakers. These are often German and tend to use the same technique as they do on the Autobahn, haring down in the outside lane flashing their lights at anyone in their way. On the loipe the lights and horn will be replaced by an 'Achtung' – though some have taken to blowing a little whistle as they charge past, weight thrust forward, and head down. Once again, though, stand your ground – make sure that if anyone is going to come a cropper, it won't be you (And don't neglect the possibility of letting a ski stick *accidentally* drift between the overtaker's legs.) It's this sort of encounter which provides yet another reason to choose to go round the loipe in the *opposite* direction to the one being taken by most people.

Incidentally, try to avoid overtaking yourself – although it is one of the rules of cross-country that no one else's speed ever coincides with yours. For if you do forge ahead of someone, it's a pretty safe bet that before long you will be overtaken by the person you passed – the old 'tortoise and the hare' syndrome.

The downhiller should find that there are certain advantages to having learnt his skiing skills on the piste. Langlaufers, for instance, tend not to be much good

at going downhill. Even something like the snow plough (elementary to most downhillers) can represent the height of technique to the langlaufer. In fact, you often see langlaufers using the lifts on the piste these days trying to get their skinny skis more used to downhill.

One of the nice things about cross-country, though, is that people tend not to be so critical of your technique, or to spend too much time developing their own. It is burning up those calories that concern them most. Of course, a few of them are starting to get the hang of the 'new' skating step – though there is a good deal of resistance to this from the traditionalists as it destroys the tracks. Thus, most continue to be content with the old kick-glide-kick diagonal stride.

So it's worth the Survival Skier trying to get a few of the more advanced techniques off-pat i.e. the skating step, fancy sidesteps from rut to rut, and, above all, that racing flick (lifting up the heel of the rear ski – even if the longest you can keep this up for is about forty metres). With any luck you should have reached the trees by then, muttering loudly to yourself as you disappear: 'Und jetzt, mit *tempo*'.

Where the downhiller can also come into his own is après-ski, or rather après-loipe. The sad fact, though, is that you may well find yourself on your own – though there's more après-loipe these days than there used to be. However, langlaufers tend to be the 'early-to-bed' type, who look down on downhillers and their after-hours cavortings as rather decadent.

○ CROSS-COUNTRY

You never get enough glide for your kick

Your degree of contempt for cross-country depends on whether you've ever done it or not

All XC trails have more uphill sections than they have level or downhill sections

Multiple trail junctions are always situated so that maximum number of langlaufers reach them at the same time

All XC clobber is either too hot while you're moving or too cold when you stop

Never believe a returning langlaufer who says the route is pretty level, or that 'You can easily do it by nightfall'

Whenever you're convinced this must be the very last bend, there'll be one more to go – at least

---

The fact is too, of course, that langlauf doesn't leave you in much shape to shake a leg of an evening. Most langlaufers tend to go either tomato red or deathly pale after their day's efforts. And it's not just your legs that go. Your stomach muscles, your torso (and also for some obscure reason your big toe) also tend to be very much the worse for wear.

So, even though 'ski de fond' may be good for you it is not exactly 'ski de fun' (which may be no bad thing for a jaded Survival Skier). It can be nice, for a change, to go to a resort that goes to bed at night.

9 SUMMER SKIING

'What do you do in the summer time?'
'I wait for the winter.'

Tycoon Roland Young to ski-instructor
Greta Garbo in *Two-faced Woman*

The one thing that could be said about skiing was that, at least, come Easter or so, it was all over for another year. You could just hang up your boots and try to forget about it. In the last few years, though, the more reluctant piste-bashers have come to the rather unsettling realisation that it is possible to ski 365 days a year — and not just on the Dendix. Even in the Alps, however, you do tend to get some funny looks from customs-officers when you roll up at the airport in August with your ski gear.

More and more glaciers are being 'rigged up' for summer skiing, and since, even in winter, summer skiing tends to be a standard conversation piece, it is something Survival Skiers should know something about. In fact, not a few Survival Skiers have actually been induced to try it out – tempted by the notion that it might be more *pleasant* to ski in your swimsuit on a warm summer's day. (And that it might provide a good excuse for opting out during the Winter.)

Certainly, there are some advantages for the Survival Skier. First, the only hotel near the glacier will be booked out and over-priced. This means you'll have to stay way down the valley in the company of a few pensioners on walking tours in a sort of Alpine ghost-town, and will thus be able to spend some hours every morning getting up to the skiing. It can actually be quite fun travelling up a series of cable cars, watching out for the marmots, spotting wild flowers and glimpsing cascading waterfalls. Fortunately, the gigantic mounds of mashed potato that form in the soft snow (to call them 'moguls' would be a euphemism) will make it impossible to ski in the afternoon – *thus limiting your skiing to half a day only.*

On the debit side, though, it does mean that you're going to have to get up at the crack of dawn – if not before – if anyone is to believe you have any serious intention of skiing. (The lifts are often open at 7 a.m.) The aim is to hit the slopes, skis chattering, while the snow is still icy hardpack, and getting in your skiing before you develop creeping paralysis of the knees, and start revealing all the deficiencies in your technique. (Unlike in the powder, in this sort of porridge you just get *stuck.*) By the way, try not to be put off by the ominous creaks and groans that you will hear from time to time as the ice shifts under the pistes. However it is not wise to venture too far off-piste in the summer – crevasses have been known to swallow ratracs, to say nothing of off-piste bashers.

Needless to say, these are not the sort of conditions in which the Survival Skier will usually perform at his best – either on the piste or at the restaurant. (There often won't be that much open in the way of poseur piazzas up on the mountain in mid-summer.) The advantage, though, is that there will be very few people around to actually take any notice of the Survival Skier's piste performance, and that glacier slopes are almost by definition open and gentle. Most of the people you find up there are die-hard ski-nuts at 'race camps' or 'ski clinics', or the members of national ski teams keeping themselves sharp and clocking one another with a stopwatch. The Survival Skier can thus spend his time admiring the view – though ski areas above the tree-line in summer do tend to look rather forlorn without their blanket of snow.

Unfortunately, there very often will not be anyone companionable to admire these views with. So much for all those ads of bikini-clad lovelies propped up on their skis, soaking up the sun. Actually these bikini pictures are all taken in the spring. (Incidentally, if you do ski in your swimsuit make sure you don't fall – snow crystals can very easily scrape off a couple of layers of tan.)

You may well find, therefore, that summer on the high peaks is simply very

often not what it is cracked up to be. For though in the winter the mountains do seem to drum up consistently clear weather, surprisingly they often fail to do so in the summer. You find it's fine and sunny down in the valley — but mist, blizzards or clouds up on the glacier (which, as we've said, can provide the Survival Skier with a reason for not going up). If you do go up in the mist, though, it does mean no one is going to be able to cast a critical eye on your performance.

Queues too tend to be in rather short supply in the summer – also somewhat unfortunate for the Survival Skier. The 'race camps' and 'clinics' seem to spend most of their time lined up on the piste discussing the technicalities of technique, fiddling with their electronic timing devices, and leaving you to go up and down the few lifts that will be working.

One tip: stay well clear of these people in the afternoons. The 'racing camp brigade' may well invite you to join them at their lectures, or video watching, or ski tuning sessions; and the individual ski nuts will want to do nothing but talk skiing, and High Factor suncreams. The latter tends to be *the* big topic of après-summer ski conversation. For though it can be icy cold in the morning, when it does heat up later the sun can easily burn a couple of layers of skin off you. Don't incidentally, miss out any bits when you apply the cream – like the tips of your ears. (They even say you should alter the position of the parting of your hair every day to ensure you don't get a line branded into your scalp.)

Summer skiing may thus have some points to commend it for the Survival Skier who wants to work on his face tan and pick wild flowers in the afternoons. He may, however, miss the camaraderie of the more jolly recreational skiers you find in the winter, and to whom most Survival Skiers' act is more specifically geared. The fact is there often isn't really anyone much up there in the summer to pose for or to perform your tricks.

○ MISHAPS

The surest way of making your tips cross is to look at them

Whenever a novice falls on a track it will be where the track is narrowest, and where it will cause the maximum inconvenience to oncoming skiers

If you schuss down into a dip, however fast you go your momentum will never be sufficient to get you up the other side without poling

The nicer a mogul looks, the more likely it is to have ice on the other side

The pocket you keep your money in is the one you always forget to zip up

If a plastic bag is blowing across an empty ski slope below you, it always moves at such a speed that at some point it will wrap itself around the tips of your skis

Just as you think no one's going to come round that corner, someone will

The part of the mogul you intended to turn on is never the bit you do turn on

---

10 SNOW WARS

'Seven times fall. Eight times get up.'

Japanese proverb

No, there's certainly no stopping them. Those Japanese have kept right on coming – in bigger and bigger numbers. And if the land of the rising yen keeps on living up to its economic reputation, it surely won't be that long before a good deal of the Alps are *owned* by Mitsubishi or some other Nipponese conglomerate.

The Japanese, of course, are not the only ones. About sixty nations now claim to be 'skiing countries'. Unfortunately though, a lot of them don't stick to sliding around at home but have taken to invading the Alps and Europe's other ski regions. All a far cry from the early decades of the century when the Brits had the slopes all to themselves – though it is true that in the very early days there were some places in the Alps where the natives would pelt the Brits engaged in their aberrant activity with stones, forcing them to confine their 'skiing-running' to moonlit nights.

The regrettable thing is that the 'stone-throwing' syndrome does seem to be coming back. And as more and more skiers crowd onto the pistes, friction between national groups has become all too common – though some of this is no more than healthy competition. Who can wear the snazziest gear? Who can turn the town upside down most effectively at night?

But all too frequently the competition is a good deal fiercer. One sign of the times, perhaps, is that last year the authorities in Zermatt introduced Switzerland's first 'Ski Police' force. Fist fights and shoving and arguing in lift-lines were apparently just some of the problems. 'They throw off their gloves and fight,' according to a senior officer. 'The Americans and English are best – they seem to know how to stand in line. But the others – Swiss, Italians, Germans, French – are not and we had problems.' Other resorts, too, are said to be trying to ban 'Pistenrowdys' from the slopes.

It's nice to see though – at least according to the Zermatt Ski Police – that the Brits are not apparently living up to their 'football hooligan' reputations. It should be pointed out though that a number of bar-owners don't seem to agree. There are some which will not admit Brits or Swedes. In fact it's those 'Big crazy Swedes' who seem to be *persona non grata* more than anyone else. They may be few in number but they certainly have made their mark off the slopes.

Perhaps this is because Brits have still not felt the need to make full use of all

those techniques honed at Highbury and Anfield. The day may come though when we will just have to display our skills with the old aerosol; or at spraying the opposition with cans of fizzed-up lager; or showing that we're a match for everyone at sliding poubelle-liners into the tips of oncoming skiers; or tripping up into a heap a group of 'enemy' skiers as they come up behind you on the lift; or dropping a well-aimed ski pole from the chairlift at some Continental Pistenjaeger flashing down between the pylons below you; or mowing down 'hostile classes' as you career into them on a kamikaze schuss; or surreptitiously 'pulling the plug' on the Walkman of the person in front of you in the queue; or jumbling up the skis of a hostile class while they're inside the restaurant at lunch (perhaps – if you have time – coating their boards with 'go slower' wax); or even – though this does seem a bit dastardly – offering your worst enemy a swig of firewater *spiked with pure alcohol* from your *other* hipflask before challenging him to a race.

The fact is, though, that xenophobia is often regarded as all part of the fun on the slopes; and any British Survival Skier worth his salt should know how to defend his national colours if need be, keeping a stiff upper lip (and weight planted *firmly* on the *lower* ski) when some foreigner comes haring down at you shouting 'Piste!', 'Achtung!', or whatever, and making sure you get your knee in his groin *first* when the inevitable collision results.

All this is undoubtedly one of the reasons why piste-bashers tend to ski more and more in their national groups. It's a form of self-protection (safety in numbers). It also perhaps explains the British preference for staying together in chalets. And on slope you can enjoy yourselves making catty remarks about the way other nations ski. However well any other national group *appears* to ski, the golden rule is to be contemptuous of their efforts. Here you will probably be aided and abetted by your instructor. (It's a growing trend to take along an instructor of your own nationality.)

Although you can happily take to task all or any of the other sixty nations sliding around on the slopes, do not, however, let anyone get away with rubbishing British skiing. Admittedly, amongst themselves, for instance, Brits may run down Cairngorm. But interrogated by any other nation you should make it clear that Cairngorm is 'fantastic'. (You can forget to mention the huge queues, lack of loos, absence of civilised cafés, uncivil service, and high prices.) No, you can tell them, Scotland is paradise compared with some of these Alpine resorts – makes you wonder why you come. And don't feel inhibited about making your views plain about some of the other skiing nations – especially when you're not directly addressing a representative of the country in question. For instance:

○ SWISS ○

A nation of goatherds and hoteliers, trying to preserve the illusion that they make money out of banking and cuckoo clocks, when really they are earning a living by overcharging you for the use of their snow.

○ AUSTRIANS ○

Pretty much the same – except that put them in a ski instructor's uniform and it's as if they were wearing jackboots.

○ ITALIANS ○

Their biggest contribution to skiing has been the pasta and pizza joints now found all over the Alps. Not to be taken seriously on the slopes though – flashy fair-weather skiers, who spend more time chatting than skiing. (Perhaps wisely as most of their ski lifts are reputed to have been obtained fifth-hand.)

○ FRENCH ○

The people we all love to hate – particularly as they now tend to be where it's at in skiing in both fashion and technology (even though they seem to spend most of their time on slope lunching). For the masochistic Brit, though, France is *the* place. If you like to have a go at the Frogs, pick somwhere like Courchevel where the locals will all look down at you. If you really want to rile them, just lay claim to 'our' boy Jean-Claude Killy, telling them that his name is really 'Kelly'. (His forebears were actually Irish Celts – not *quite* British, but near enough.)

○ **GERMANS** ○

A bunch of langlaufers rather than skiers. 'Schwobs' as the Swiss would say abusively or 'Piefkes' as the Austrians call them. And you surely can't call the Zugspitze and its surroundings a skiing area. Anyway it all seems to have been leased out to the US army.

Another point to bear in mind is that even in resorts where the Brits are a majority, always pretend that you are being over-run – the K-factor (Krauts), the F-factor (Frogs), not to mention the S-factor (Sloanes). A good line to take is that Pistendorf was so much nicer before that other lot arrived. Nor should you make any attempt to pronounce the local names correctly – thus Saulze D'Oulx becomes Sowsy (or 'Saucy screw' as some would have it), Meribel becomes Maybel, and St. Moritz becomes Morrers.

Of course, we all have our own national characteristics and that is what makes the ski scene interesting. Brits, for instance, have this habit of wearing their swimsuits in the sauna, but are the first to strip off on the slopes. To non-Europeans, of course, all this may seem a bit daunting. They may not realise that inter-European aggro is all part of the fun, and has been for centuries, and that we actually *enjoy* this sort of thing. So how are those other nations who are now beginning to appear amongst us in ever greater numbers going to fit in – notably the Japanese and the Americans?

○ **JAPANESE** ○

In a way it's a pity the Japanese have had to come to terms with this unruly scene. The ones we have seen so far have seemed to be a disciplined gentle bunch – though we shouldn't forget they too have their crazy side: the term 'Kamikaze skier' wasn't coined for nothing; and it was of course Yuichiro Miura (now director of Sapporo Ski School) who schussed down Everest (with the aid of a parachute) in 1970.

Make no mistake though, they are making inroads – especially where gear and clobber is concerned (and that, as we've seen, is really what it's all about). Even French moniteurs have now been equipped with Descente suits. And YKK, of course, is the biggest manufacturer of zips in the world. Their gear, though, does tend to be pretty flash – even changing colour according to the temperature. And when it comes to really 'flash trash', they must surely be way ahead with their new 'disposable' cameras. Fortunately, they haven't yet got the hang of making good skis – though they have put up the trade barriers to prevent European and American imports.

Once on the planks, as you might expect, they don't give up easily, and they

tend to keep bashing away from dawn to dusk. One problem is that you very often don't see them coming — not last year anyway when they had a penchant for white ski suits. And since they do tend to be rather small, you could have a whole class of them through your legs before you knew what hit (or hopefully) missed you.

An indication of the extent of their obsession with skiing is the 'urban slalom' building being put up in Tokyo — a six-storey refrigerated building in the city complete with spiral slopes, three lifts and nine artificial snow machines.

So don't underestimate them. They are pretty well bound to get there in the end and they are prepared to take their time about it. Japan itself is reputed on weekends to have the longest ski lift queues in the world and the largest concentration of skiers (twelve million plus). (They may perhaps just be the Ultimate Survival Skiers — and we may in time be able to learn from them.)

The ones you will come across in the Alps, though, will tend to keep very much to themselves — like everyone else, skiing in national groups — and going through their exercises in rigid formation, rather like the Austrians, often all

dressed the same with a big brand name on their outfits, carrying a small backpack – *and apparently eager not to cause trouble.*

Let's try to keep it that way – misunderstandings can so easily occur. When they talk about 'Yuki', for instance, they mean 'snow' – not that they think Euro-snow is yukky. There's also that mysterious 'Wa' they're always on about, which apparently translates as 'harmony'. So don't misunderstand a Nip hurtling down the mountain murmuring 'Wa' under his breath. He is not making a declaration of war and there would not normally be any need to fear imminent attack. Just say politely, 'Ah ha! wa' (though apparently it isn't done to talk about 'wa' since it then disappears). And this might upset him.

○ THE AMERICANS ○

You'd have thought the fall in the dollar would have kept their numbers down. But it doesn't seem to – any more than the falling pound has been deterring Brits from getting their annual winter fix in the Alps. And like those gentle Japanese, they must also experience a certain culture shock when they find themselves pitched into European-style 'snow wars'.

The thing is that 'stateside' skiing, whilst very 'macho', is also an altogether more friendly business – wishing one another frequently 'Have a nice day', rather than the European 'Out of my way'. Americans don't even seem to have heard of jumping the queue (or rather 'not standing in line'), or jostling on the T-bar (perhaps because they're more used to chairs). And instead of spending their time fighting for elbow room and unsettling their partner on the drag-lift, they just introduce themselves (despite the name badge on their anorak if they are part of a group), and settle down to tell you their life-story, wishing you cheerfully 'A good day's skiing' when you get to the top.

And they really seem to mean it. Americans, it seems, do come to *ski* rather than to pose (as evidenced by their gear). Like the Japanese they too seem to have come to Europe for some ultimate skiing experiences – though they are not so much looking for 'Wa' as for runs that will 'Wow' them. They do have a rather disconcerting habit of yipping at the tops of their voices whenever these 'Wow' experiences occur and they find themselves airborne coming off the top of a bump made of some of that European 'white gold'.

No less than with other nations, though, there is the problem of the language barrier. Americans are forever heading back to 'the lodge' or to the 'condo' (while we all go back to our hotels and apartments); or waiting for 'trams' (perhaps they use those over there instead of 'cable cars'); or hitting the 'trail' (as they set out to bash the 'piste'). Even their well-intentioned warnings are not much help as they call out to you 'Watch out for the tiller', just as a ratrac is about to mow you down; or calling out 'timber' or 'track' instead of 'Get out of my way. I am out of control'.

The only time they can get a bit touchy is when you start making unfavourable comparisons with US skiing. Admittedly they are over here because the Alps are a sort of snow-worshippers' Mecca. But when it comes to Vail versus Saint Moritz, or American powder versus European powder, they certainly aren't going to concede defeat. And as for that 'European ambiance', well there's more than something to be said for good old 'down home' US skiing.

Like the Japanese, they too are making inroads. Europe still seems to be ahead in equipment. But the Americans are the ones who invented modern snow — the stuff shot out of a cannon. (It's thanks to them that Europeans will probably now be able to go skiing in December again; and also the fact that there are more and more Kleenex dispensers at the bottom of the slopes at modern resorts to wipe your goggles.)

Let's just hope it doesn't go too far and we find ourselves sustaining ourselves on slope on hamburgers, beer and popcorn rather than saucisson, pâté and white wine, or that, like them, we start spending 'Happy Hour' in gigantic parking lots at the foot of the slopes with stuff from the picnic cooler, rather than in some good old European steamy Stübli.

○ ACHES AND PAINS

The chills and spills will outnumber the thrills

Falling is more fun when someone else does it

It is more painful when someone else is watching

If your leg breaks it won't be in a way they know how to fix at the resort

You won't discover this 'till you get home

Flying through the air with the greatest of ease is a lot simpler than landing

The side of your body on which you fall is always the side with the pocket in which you have both your keys and your sunglasses

It's when you're going your best that the worst will happen

If you don't get skier's thumb, you'll get skier's toe

---

11 APRÈS-SKI

**'Keep it simple. Don't eat too much, don't drink too much,
and don't smoke too much – but don't do too little
of them either.'**

Hermann 'Jackrabbit' Smith-Johannsen,
who skied till he was 105 and died at 111

As pointed out in *Piste Again*, on-slope activities are not exactly the most compatible with off-slope activities. And it takes a hardened Survival Skier to keep his end up at both. In recent years, if anything, things have got worse, to the extent that it's almost *impossible* to do both – unless you pick a resort with one ski lift and six discos or, alternatively, a resort which is famous for the *non*-existence of its night-life.

Sadly, though, there are fewer and fewer of these places about. At the bigger resorts there's now hardly anything that's *not* on offer après-ski. They've all got massive sports complexes with swimming pools, tennis, squash, aerobics, yoga, ice skating, shooting galleries, golf driving-ranges, courses in this, that and the other, floodlit skiing, and all manner of bars, dives and night spots for whatever your taste – Schuhplattler, knobbly knees contests, snow dances, hell-raising, wood-chopping, disco-raving, bar-hopping or just plain hard drinking. Far from being 'dolce far niente', après-ski is now very much 'dolce far *molto*'. And this is perhaps the explanation for the growth of the poseur-phenomenon we mentioned earlier. It's just about the only way of ensuring you still have the legs for what happens 'après-piste'.

One problem is that these days après-ski is getting going *far too early* – if you are going to stay the course through to the small hours that is. First, there's the now established phenomenon of the extended lunch on the slopes, after which it's considered quite normal to head straight for one of the après-piste bars at the foot of the slopes. Thus we find ourselves nipping in for 'a quick one' *as early as 4 p.m.* to rub noses, thaw out and start exchanging lies about what we did that day. (This can even be a bit too soon for the most quick-thinking Survival Skier to have got his stories sorted out.)

Inevitably, of course, the quick one usually turns into a quick one *or three*. And so, against our better judgement we head for another smoky cave for 'real drinkers'; or to a dance-bar to work off the effects by dancing in our ski boots. (God knows ski boots are hard enough to walk in – let alone dance in.) The result is that after a few more grogs at Pub 21, and Pub 37 and then Pub 45 (or

was it 46?) – Alpine pubs so often seem to be numbered – you head for your chalet or hotel with your double-glazed eyes (no you didn't forget to take your goggles off), your mouth tasting like the inside of a ski instructor's glove, and your head like the inside of a telephone exchange (and no – it wasn't your Walkman that was playing up). Incidentally, the Survival Skier would be well advised to do his après-piste drinking at the *bottom* of the slopes – not at those bars halfway up the slope, where you will then have to *ski* the rest of the way down.

Now all this wouldn't be so bad if you could just go back and sleep it off in the sauna, and then clear your head with a bit of walkabout before dinner – the good old promenade through the village, visiting the ski shop and the supermarket, and doing a bit of celebrity-spotting, or sitting in a café over an ice-cream and hot chocolate. The problem is that the locals have got it into their heads that what their visitors want straight apre-piste is *even more* physical jerks – not the old Apfelstrudel and thé citron at the local Konditorei. So they've been investing like crazy in all those sports facilities we mentioned earlier – in an effort, it would seem, to finish us off for good.

The Survival Skier, unfortunately, with his reputation to think of, will not be able to opt out of this session completely. After all, his performance as a skier will often be judged by the showing he makes après-ski. So try not to clutch your aching limbs too obviously when you climb out of the jacuzzi; and don't stagger, red-faced and lank-haired out of the sauna saying 'I can't take it anymore'. Stick, however, to this sort of activity rather than to a couple of sets of squash or a quick game of ice hockey. Leave that to the ski hooligans who enjoy bashing foreigners and who have brought their hurling sticks along. Survival Skiers will probably prefer to spend this time inspecting their bruises rather than acquiring more.

As far as the rest of the evening goes, the Survival Skier should find he is rather better prepared. He should, for instance, have spent the off-season eating three to four big meals a day, and bending the old elbow at frequent intervals in order to get in shape for his holiday. (This won't however leave you looking your best for 'strip fondue' – drop a piece of meat, and drop a piece of clothing.) In fact even ordinary fondue is probably better avoided; there's always that frustration of dropping bits back in just as you get them out, and then chasing in vain the last piece of bread skidding around in the bottom of the pot.

By this stage of the evening, though, the Survival Skier should have got his stories of the day's exploits on the slopes sorted out – so that they seem almost plausible – or at least as plausible as anyone else's. Thus he should be a match for any of the black run bores over the old raclette and plonk particularly as by now he will probably be hungry enough to eat his ski socks and polish off his inner-soles for dessert. And, with any luck, you will be served up something that slides down even better.

It's after dinner though that the Survival Skier will have to show that he can really cut the mustard. The fact is that even if you are not at Saint Moritz, all skiers will be expected to put in an 'après-ski' show. And after staring death in the face all day, a lot of people like to get their own back by dressing to kill at night. So, you'll be decked out in your après-ski ensemble (smart or unsmart according to where you are) – perhaps in your crocodile skin ski pants and diamond-studded moonboots. (Fortunately moonboots, like ski boots, have now also gone hi-tech and the new type of undersole should help you to stay upright.) If you've still got the mammoth's foot type, the dress-conscious Survival Skier will, of course, have fluffed them up them with a hair-dryer. These days there are even après-ski skis – small rubber jobs. But you'd probably be safer in your moonboots or your wellies or perhaps on a pair of snow shoes instead.

The Survival Skier who will get the most out of the evening is the one who can enhance his on-slope reputation by now going in for the sort of activities that would appear to require a certain amount of skiing ability. This is your big

chance to make your reputation *on* the slopes *off* the slopes (as well as providing a handy excuse for not appearing the next day – if things don't go quite as intended.)

So you might just think of volunteering for the:

– torchlight skiing party. (Despite the 'torchlight' it should be too dark to spot your skiing inadequacies.)

– the candlelight toboggan race. (Being well tanked up is the main qualification for this – so you should be OK.)

– the moonlight snow-dance. (You don't actually have to do it on skis – even those little rubber ones.)

– skiing in fancy dress by floodlight. (If you're suitably disguised i.e. totally unrecognisable, you can always pretend afterwards that *you* were the masked 'mystery' figure who skied like a dream and then disappeared.)

– bar-hopping on skis. (You can probably manage this if the bars aren't too far apart from one another – preferably adjoining.)

Don't however get too carried away in your choice of activity – jumping over barrels on ice skates, for instance, is harder than it looks.

Having now established your reputation, you can start to have some *real* fun. After all, the night is still young. Now's your chance to go to the sort of places and to do the sort of things which you would take infinite pains to avoid at home. So take your pick – head for the Pferdestall, or Bierkeller, or Club 77 or Five-to-Five Bar for whatever takes your fancy: 'Hot Legs' contests; moonbooted

---

○ NOSH

The higher you eat, the higher the price and the less haute the cuisine

The chances of you banana-skidding in your ski boots on the tiled floor of the mountain cafeteria, increases in direct proportion to the amount of food you are carrying on your tray

The number of calories consumed at the après-ski tea or booze-up will be at least double the number of calories burned up during the day's piste-bashing

Ski-slope meals are better at getting your stomach moving than your skis moving

There's always a queue for the loo

The piste map is harder to read after a good lunch

If there was some stale bread and hard cheese left in the morning, it'll be fondue that evening

---

congas; hokey-kokeys; passing hot potatoes around between your legs (in the nude if you're doing it properly); some *real* 'snow' – the imported variety that you sniff at chic resorts. (Anything seems to go in après-ski these days – you even find transvestite floorshows in some resorts.)

Chances are though that you'll probably find yourself doing the 'flake-out flop' to an electronic zither or 'Ländler Band', in some sweaty dive, working up a thirst for Stein after foaming Stein. Either that, or some *real* hell-raising, wearing lampshades on your head, putting fondue down other people's shirts – the sort of thing, in fact, that puts the 'Hooray' into Henry.

The locals have actually now begun to realise that there is less interest than there was in the folksy side – Schuhplattler, flag-waving, Alpenhorn-blowing, and so on – and more interest in getting a real skinful of concoctions that you wouldn't dream of pouring down your neck at home: Jägertee, chisky (cherry brandy and whisky), snakebite (a lethal brew of beer, cider and vodka drunk by the pint), spiked vin chaud (in half pint mugs), cocktails made out of whatever the barman has left over, or perhaps one of the 'Cresta' classics like Bullshot (vodka and consommé, well-chilled). In short, the kind of concoctions that gave an international notoriety a couple of years ago to that bar in Denmark where the landlord would serve up his customers with his own dastardly 'special' – at the same time getting his customer to bare his behind for a belt on the arse, (the idea being that this was a drink with a real 'sting in the tail').

This certainly seems to be the direction ski resorts are heading – ensuring you get enough lethal liquor down your throat so that you can hardly push open those heavy Alpine doors for a final bout of mayhem on the way home, crashing your electric trolley or your toboggan or your bin-liner a few times en route, whilst performing a few other gratuitous acts of violence along the way (nicking roadsigns, lighting fires etc.), and perhaps stopping off for a visit to the crêperie or for some Bratwurst and chips. (Skiers tend to be at their hungriest at 4.30 a.m. and 4.30 p.m.)

Of course, you can just stay in and play chess, go to a skiing lecture or a concert, play with the computer (some big hotels are even offering these now), attend a course in photography or Alpine flowers, or have a quiet game of scrabble. Incidentally, don't on any account take on the locals at space invaders, or 'mini-foot' (i.e. table football) – you'll come off a worse loser than you would at one of the more hairy activities we outlined.

But no Survival Skier worthy of the name should be seen to opt out like this. And, painful as it may be, après-ski does *just* beat staying in your room boozing out of a toothmug. Anyway, you've little choice. As we've said, if you can't exactly cut the mustard *on* the slopes, you've got to show you can hack it *off* the slopes. And with any luck, it won't be too long before the Japanese take over. Apparently, their idea of après-ski is a Japanese bath and a spot of shinto-worship.

○ COMPANIONS

An 'experienced' skier is someone who got to the resort one day before you did

The likelihood of someone talking about tip-rolls and gut-flips is in inverse proportion to his ability to perform them

The skier you most want to avoid is the one you are most likely to bump into – literally

The size of a chalet party bears no relation to the size of the chalet

If you meet the romance of your life on the T-bar and spend the journey up discovering how much you have in common, chances are that when you get to the top you'll find that what you don't have in common is skiing ability

The best opportunity you will ever have to inspect the nostrils of people you don't know will be in the 9.15 a.m. cable-car

The chalet girl is having a better holiday than you are

---

12 SUMMIT MEETINGS

**'People say it's piste-bashing by day
and duvet-bashing all night.'**

Ski-bum quoted in *New Society*

Many skiers spend a good deal of the year getting into shape – trying to get that skier's body. Once on the slopes, though, it's often more a question of how to get that *other* skier's body – and that also goes for a fair number of Survival Skiers. If you've studied the previous chapter, though, you may wonder if you'd be in any position to do anything with that other body if you did manage to get at it.

Nevertheless, skiing romances do still seem to take place and this prospect is probably still one of the main reasons for going. The very term 'ski lodge' with images of being cosily curled up in front of a log-fire for two is almost synonymous with romance (although today's multi-occupancy chalets have rather destroyed that Hollywood illusion). Also, of course, the majority of skiers are single. (Why on earth then do Americans have to have those 'singles' snow-weeks?)

Certainly, as we've seen, people do tend to shed their inhibitions while skiing – whether it's playing 'strip fondue' or getting together in mixed saunas. And although most people (well some) are looking for good clean fun on the slopes, it's often good *dirty* fun they're looking for after sunset – not just a waltz round the ice-rink and a foxtrot at the tea dance. (These, surprisingly, are coming back into style by the way – despite the absence of people under thirty who can foxtrot.) The line here for the amorously inclined Survival Skier is: 'We don't seem to be terribly good at this – perhaps we could do something else together.' Or: 'Neither skiing nor dancing is the best aerobic work-out, you know.'

After all, it does make sense. To quote a reply recently given to a British reporter who asked a girl from Alaska how she managed to cope with those harsh dark days of winter: 'I find someone nice and stay indoors.' The problem is, as always, the 'finding someone nice'; and the odds are rather against the males who tend to heavily outnumber the girls on the slopes. The Survival Skier, however, should start with certain advantages – given the dash he probably cuts on the piste. In the end, surely, all that posing practice should pay off.

The snag, though, is that it's not always easy to see what there is underneath all those layers of ski wear. Of course, personality is a lot more important than looks – but there are limits. This, incidentally, is one of the few advantages of

summer skiing – on the one day the sun shines all will be revealed. And you can offer to smooth some of that factor 20 suncream all over him or her – especially in those delicate parts. Furthermore, summer skiing does leave you free in the afternoon. . . .

In winter, though, the Survival Skier's best bet is probably the swimming-pool, the sauna or the jacuzzi if you want to check out what you might be getting ('Who's got the biggest knockers/biggest dong?' is actually one of the standard après-ski games.) Fortunately, sauna hour is usually early enough in the evening so that, if necessary, you can suddenly remember that you had other plans. If all seems well, on the other hand, you can then offer to take his or her pulse, or offer a little gentle toning up on the massage table: 'The thighs do tend to get so tensed up during skiing, don't you find?'

Skiers incidentally do tend to have fairly meaty thighs – especially powderhounds, or heli-skiers, who are the real 'thigh guys'. So if you're a real Survival Skier (i.e. you hardly do it at all) it might be best to decline an offer to reciprocate. Otherwise your potential partner may begin to suss that you're not actually all that you seem. Out on the slope, though, the Survival Skier should be

able to *seem* as if he or she might be just the job to team up with for a little after-hours pole-planting.

Do make sure, though, that you set up your liaisons *on* the slopes. Expecting to meet that special someone après-ski is a non-starter. To the Survival Skiing male it may often *seem* that there are more bumps and curves parked on the barstools in the village than on the slopes – but these usually belong to chalet girls who won't be interested in *him*. And most ski resort discos are so dark and awful that there's no telling whom you may be leaving with, or of what sex (and these days you can't be too careful).

The great advantage of the slopes is that you do meet on neutral ground and there are plenty of opportunities for those 'chance' encounters – perhaps engineering discreet collisions and offering to help put his or her skis back on. (Incidentally, the Survival Skier should try to make it look like the other person's fault – he doesn't want to make himself out to be a worse skier than he is.) If you actually can ski, of course, then you can just cruise over and say: 'Do you fall down often:' or 'Isn't this the life?' If the reply is 'Not with you around', you picked the wrong victim. It's also easier on the slopes to get a conversation going – unlike at the disco you can usually hear one another.

The Survival Skier's big advantage is his sincerity. Given his general disinterest in skiing, he or she can genuinely look into his prospective partner's eyes on a mountain top as if his new friend was the most important thing in the world – on that particular mountain anyway. The Survival Skier should not forget the importance of flattery. Make sure you say that he/she is 'looking good'. They'll really appreciate it. (After all, the outfit did cost £500.)

With his skill at getting around the slopes the Survival Skier should also have a headstart. In your case, though, it will tend to be a case of appearing *alongside* at the right moments, rather than getting round yourself in full view of your partner – particularly if he or she is a better skier than you.

Not that incompatibility of skiing levels need necessarily be a major barrier to romance. In the unlikely event that you're the stronger party, this enables you to offer a little personal advice and tuition. And if you're the weaker – well, it's surprising how much other skiers can enjoy taking you under their wing. Some Survival Skiers even pretend to be even more incompetent than they really are and find that this works wonders. But this is perhaps not to be recommended if you're a male trying to seduce the local snow queen.

Far better, though, to find yourselves close to one another in the lift queue treading on one another's skis ('Do you always jump the queue?') Even better perhaps is the cable car queue, where your towering extra-long skis should make quite an impression. Should you find yourself sharing a t-bar or a gondola with him or her, there are all manner of possibilities for breaking the ice – although with today's new super-fast lifts you do get less time than you did.

You can, for instance, offer a listen on your Walkman from your spare

earphone (try to remember to wipe off the earwax of the previous person you loaned it to); or share your blanket on the double chair – who knows, you may soon be picnicking together on it; or you can offer any number of the other little bits and pieces from your bum-bag – your 'hand warmer', your suntan lotion ('What a lovely colour you are – you just need a splash of this to get the shade absolutely perfect'). The fact that this person undoubtedly has a similar supply of bits and pieces about his or her person does seem to indicate that if he or she accepts, this could be the start of something.

You can then feel pretty sure that he or she won't take it amiss when you rub the snow off his or her bottom on alighting from the lift; or help him or her off the t-bar with a little shove on the behind – particularly if you have been rubbing boots together all the way up the t-bar. (One tip though for the Survival Skier – t-bars do tend to attract foot fetishists; so bear this in mind when you are scouting out the lift lines.)

But even if your relationship is at an even more advanced stage, it does pay not to get too carried away on the ski lift. An embrace on the t-bar can leave you in a nasty tangle indeed. Even the arm round the shoulders can have unforeseen consequences – unless you actually want to roll back down to the bottom of the slope intertwined. A similar fate is likely to befall you if you and your beloved rashly take out one of those mono boards for couples – at least if *one* of you is a Survival Skier.

Better to leave all that groping until you meet for lunch. Here on the terra firma of the restaurant there should be no hazards in helping one another to peel off those clothes and undo one another's boots – with probably mounting curiosity and excitement on both sides as you get closer to discovering what exactly lies beneath. Another tip here for the Survival Skier: Don't forget to wear silk next to your skin – it does feel so sexy if your friend does get his or her fingers to it.

So far we have tended to concentrate on getting the gear *off*. But that, of course, can be to diminish the role of clothing on the slopes. After all, as we said in the opening chapters, the object of ski wear and skiing is to be a sex object – never mind the burnt skin, peeling nose and chapped lips. And the clothes can be used to send all manner of sexual signals. The Survival Skier would do well to study these carefully in order not to make any nasty errors. For instance, leaving your bandanna undone tends to mean 'Come here and knot it for me'; whereas wrapped around tight and knotted behind usually means you are unavailable.

Needless to say, the Survival Skier should keep his actual performance on slope to a minimum from now on – unless he wants to undo all his good work. Skiing ability is so often equated with sexual performance. If necessary, try to ski in another group. And women should, on no account, ski in a higher class than their spouses. (The problem is that, as at dancing, women often make better skiers.)

It's when you get off the slopes that things are going to get more difficult.

What with the sardine-syndrome in much ski-lodging, hardly anyone has a room to themselves any more; and you will also probably feel obliged to put in a bit of après-ski – which, as we saw in the previous chapter, doesn't leave you in much shape for anything else. One word of advice here: stay away from the Ski Instructor's Ball – if you want to hang on to your partner.

A good Survival Skiing line in order to cut back on the après-ski, and also making you seem like a bit of an old hand at the skiing game is: 'I can remember the days when we had to make our own après-ski.' (Nudge, nudge). You could then suggest a romantic midnight toboggan ride, or a horsedrawn sleigh for two, or a stroll down a lamplit path for winter walks as you head for even more intimate togetherness.

Thereafter, things may be a little less romantic. Stepping through piles of smelly socks and puddles of vomit to your corner of the chalet, or sneaking up a creaky stairway in a mountain pension to a bed with more lumps than a mogul field is hardly an auspicious start to any après-après-ski. Your room or hers – it'll probably be just as bad.

You may, however, earn your partner's respect for being able to make love in some pretty unorthodox positions — one leg on the radiator, simultaneously wrestling with the 'thermo-bot' you brought with you in case the radiator clapped out, doing your best not to put your foot in the mouth of the person in the bed next to you (despite his snoring), and writhing around as if you're wedeling (as those bedsprings press into your spine.)

○ APRÈS-SKI

The moguls get bigger as the day goes on — and bigger still when you get to the bar

By lunch-time you will have had enough

By the end of the afternoon you will have had more than enough

At the end of the day it will hurt even where it didn't during the day

The people with the highest profile at the bar will have the lowest profile on the slopes

The après-ski action is always somewhere else

At the end of the day there is always someone who has skied further or steeper

The best après-ski activity of all is going home

---

13 SKIING DOUBLE

**'They have style, the best of these
high altitude drunkards.'**

Robert Schultheis, on Tibetan folk in
Mountain Gazette

Après-ski *on* the slopes has become an increasingly worrying phenomenon. Forty per cent of skiing accidents in Austria last year were attributed to drinking (so the title of this book 'Totally Piste' is not entirely inapt).

The Survival Skier, of course should always be wary of *other* skiers who get out of control because of alcohol. But he should be equally wary of the 'piste-police' trying to crack down on his own boozing. After all, the reason many of us go is to get 'more piste for our pound'. And, as we've seen, most Survival Skiers need as much Dutch courage as they can get and are not in the habit of relying on St Bernard dogs for their brandy supply. Thus, they are often not exactly innocent parties themselves in those late afternoon collisions.

The Americans, incidentally, are getting the right idea. Some resorts now have teams of 'Thirstbusters', wearing taxi-cab yellow jumpsuits, who cruise the slopes with special patented back-packs that dispense hot apple cider and cocoa for a buck a pop.

The fact is that most Survival Skiers often find themselves more in need of moral fortification on the slopes than of the sexual gratification we discussed in the last chapter. The Survival Skier may not exactly have 'bottle' but he usually has 'a bottle' (or two) – not just to refuel (you burn up a lot of calories ducking around the slopes) but to offer to all those pisteurs he needs to keep in with, ensuring they come up at appropriate moments with reputation-building remarks like: 'That must be the tenth time this morning you came down the Black Buzzard.'

It would also be a pity – not least for the Survival Skier – if the tradition of the odd wee nip as you get around the slopes were to be outlawed. It's a tradition that goes a lot further back than Survival Skiing. There's hardly a high mountain range in the world where for centuries mountain men have not been putting away some special lethal liquid down their cast-iron stomachs to keep them going – jealously guarding the secrets of their fermentation methods from the lowlanders (and the law). And the same goes for the Alps – whether it be Zwetsch, Weinbrand, Mirabelle, Pflümli, Obstler or some more deadly form of 'anti-freeze' like Neaule. And what about all those piste-side Stübli or other watering holes – do we want to put them out of business? Let's not pretend we just go there to listen to the instructor tell us what we had been doing wrong; we go for the grog, and then more grog – preferably served in half-pint mugs.

But as well as providing an often much-needed form of central heating, Survival Skiers and others do find that a little lubrication *helps* their skiing. You often tend to be at your most adventurous after a couple of Jägertees to round off your lunch. (There must be a reason why so many of those bars are called 'Whiskey-*a-go-go*'.) How often have you heard people emerge from the restaurant at 3.30 p.m. and (after spending half an hour or so trying to locate their sticks and poles) pronounce: 'I always ski so much better after a good lunch.'

After all, isn't that what the instructors have all been telling us since way back – that the secret is to ski 'relaxed'. Even cross-country instructors (altogether a more puritanical sort) are always calling out 'locker bleiben' ('Stay loose'). The fact of the matter is that if the hipflask were passed around on the slopes a bit more frequently there would be no need for all those weird ways devised by the 'inner skiing' schools to help you relax.

It's also true that in skiing, as in anything else, you have to make the most of your natural assets. And since most Survival Skiers have spent years of their lives developing hollow legs, it seems a shame not to use them. Perhaps, in time, who knows, they'll get as rubbery and flexible as those of your instructor.

Not that this is a theory to which your instructor will all that often subscribe; though like most mountain men, they are not usually averse to a bit of a nip themselves – particularly if it's the Survival Skier who is passing the hipflask around. ('After all, it's always five o'clock somewhere.') If you do this often enough, you may not become the best skier in the group, but you'll almost certainly be the most popular.

It's something of a pity then – not least for the Survival Skier – that the authorities are trying to cut down on pit-stops at piste-side hostelries or those breaks on the slopes for a little noggin. One does wonder whether they have considered the medical consequences – many a skier trapped on a mountain has just managed to avoid succumbing to hypothermia by having a hip flask handy, as well as using it as an antiseptic. Admittedly there is now a school of thought that alcohol can cause a *loss* of bodyheat and in itself induce hypothermia. But Survival Skiers (who tend to rely on their own experience) would be advised to dismiss this as just another modern theory and rely instead on their own experience and that of 'fellow' mountain men over the ages.

So it does seem rather a pity that Survival Skiers have now been reduced to buying those hollow-shafted ski-poles to surreptitiously carry their booze around in. (If you drop one of these from the ski lift, of course, then you've *really* got something to worry about.) Nor will these poles do anything for your skiing – especially for someone like the Survival Skier, whose equipment needs to be so *delicately* balanced: a litre of firewater washing around inside your sticks can destroy your rhythm entirely. (One tip worth remembering: try to empty each shaft evenly so that you stay roughly in balance.)

In some respects, though, it must be admitted that the authorities do have a point. There have been cases where people didn't just drop their stick on top of someone from the chairlift: having consumed the contents of their sticks they fell off the chairs themselves onto skiers below. That's 'vertical drop' for you.

Fortunately, however, a satisfactory solution seems to be emerging – both to the piste police and to skiers who enjoy a tincture or two in the afternoon. The key to this is the 'long lunch' which, thanks largely to the French and the Italians has now become an established phenomenon on the slopes. Understandably these lunches tend to be mainly of the liquid variety – since though food at the top of the mountain has got better, it often seems a bit 'tired', as if it had made a big effort to get up there.

Survival Skiers need only refine this brilliant concept a bit further, and it should be possible to virtually eliminate the need to do any more skiing for the rest of the day. (If queried, of course, don't blame this on your well-filled hollow legs – say instead that you're 'very sensitive' to the 'flat light' situation that seems to occur so often in the afternoon, impeding visibility and making the bumps look flat.)

Then, with your ski clips undone you can simply catch the cable car down.

Better that — and more congenial — than sitting up on the slope boozing and waiting for the piste-patrol to bring you down. With a bit of practice, the concept could perhaps be refined even further — extending your après-ski to dawn and then staying off the slopes (in the best interests of all concerned, since with a hangover your skiing is likely to be somewhat erratic at best).

And don't believe that one about a blast of cold air being the best cure for a hangover. As we've seen, medical science seems to be overturning a lot of these old theories; with any luck they'll now recommend you to stay in bed with a little warm Jägertee. Perhaps it all just goes to prove the central philosophy of the *'Piste'* series — that the best way to succeed at skiing is to do your own thing.